L T :

A STREET COP'S STORIES

L T :
A STREET COP'S STORIES

By
Lt. Ernie W. Hinkle, Jr., Retired

With Elizabeth M. Hinkle

L T: A Street Cop's Stories

ISBN: 1499529686
ISBN-13: 9781499529686

Edited by Mike Cox and Elizabeth Hinkle

Cover photos by Joel Todd Smith

Cartoons by William Beechinor

Formatted by Ann Bell

Published by Katy Crossing Press
300 Katy Crossing
Georgetown, TX 78626
www.katycrossingpress.com
annamaebell@yahoo.com

Katy Crossing Press

To Elizabeth, my wife, who has
been the force behind this book
– my guiding light.

Preface

For most of my 35 years with the Austin Police Department, I worked the streets. During that time, I rose in rank from rookie patrolman to sergeant to lieutenant. Like all officers, I had a wide range of experience from seeing tragedies first hand and surviving my own close calls to being the butt of practical jokes.

After I retired, I began to realize it was important to write down some of my stories for my family and, maybe in doing so, provide a few laughs and hopefully some insight to younger and future officers. Many of my stories show the sacrifices that dedicated officers make.

If I have made any mistakes with names or events, please remember that I relied almost solely on my memory. Most of the time I used real names; but, in some cases where using a name might reopen an old wound, I left it out. For those folks with little to be proud of, I've given either nicknames or mentioned no name at all.

Truly, I have worked with some of the finest people (police officers and support staff, citizens, federal, state, and county agencies) you could ever meet. The officers often worked on holidays, weekends, nights, and many times had to spend their off days in court without being paid for it. They were committed to protecting Austin's citizens from danger.

That said, I would like to point out that there is nothing special about me. A sharecropper's son from Kentucky, I was just one street cop trying to be the best officer I could be. A risk taker but not a thrill seeker, a cop with a genuine desire to protect and serve the citizens of my city, I was proud to be an Austin police officer.

I hope you enjoy reading these stories as much as I enjoyed my career serving the people of Austin.

Lt. Ernie Hinkle, Retired

Acknowledgments

I want to thank my wife, Elizabeth "Beth" Hinkle for her dedication and the endless amount of time she spent trying to make sense of my handwriting as I put these stories down on paper. Without her, this book would never have been finished—maybe not even started.

Thanks also to my family for their continual encouragement for me to preserve some of the stories they had heard me tell over the years.

Special thanks go to the men and women I have worked with, the Austin Police Department, and the citizens of Austin for allowing me the opportunity to serve them. You have put a lot of faith in your police officers and I tried to do my best.

And, last but not least, I thank Mike Cox, who I have known for more than 40 years, for his editing assistance and guidance and Ann Bell for her publishing assistance.

"Blessed is the man who walks not in the counsel of the wicked—he is like a tree planted by streams of water."
Psalms: 1: 1-3

TABLE OF CONTENTS

Dedication
Preface
Acknowledgements

PICTURES LETTERS AND AWARDS

THE BEGINNING

My Old Kentucky Home

I spent most of my working life in law enforcement but, looking back, I came close to becoming a bootlegger just like my Uncle Parker.

Born in Hopkinsville, Kentucky in 1932 at the height of the Great Depression, I have one sister, Carolyn, who is six years younger. My parents were hardworking people and instilled that trait in me. The fourth grade was the extent of both of my parents' education. Dad was a sharecropper and Mother worked at the local Laundromat. Later, Dad got a job as a custodian at the Belmont Grade School in Hopkinsville and worked there until he was 80.

On weekends when I was a boy, my uncle, Parker West, would often come by and pick me and my family up and take us to Uncle John's farm at Honey Grove. My mother's brothers and sisters would also often be there. They would all work together canning fruits and vegetables, killing and processing hogs, and the men would go squirrel hunting. Our family was very close-knit and loving. During the summer, I stayed at the farm to work in the tobacco field. I would also sell watermelons alongside the main road.

I still have first cousins in Hopkinsville and we enjoy visiting with them when we can. They all have special, fun-loving children and grandchildren.

When I was a kid, all of our family were poor and had very little. Uncle Parker did a lot to help support our family, but not everything he did was exactly legal. He was crippled, but he would fight at the drop of a hat. For that, he spent some time in jail. Unfortunately, when he got out, he would do the same thing all over again.

A bootlegger, Uncle Parker made a fairly good living during those times by driving a "tanker." A tanker is a car equipped to carry moonshine. His was a 1932 Ford coupe with a tank built under the step sides and in the rumble seat.

The woods hid many a still and also were full of squirrels. As a boy, I spent a lot of time in the woods hunting squirrels. Once, when I was about eleven, I was deep in the sticks when I

Ernie Hinkle

walked up on an automobile that was hidden in a ditch and covered with brush. I had found me a car! I ran to find Uncle John to share the good news. He was in the tobacco field when I found him and I told him about it. He said, "That is Uncle Parker's car and it is hot, so he is hiding it out." Uncle John told me not to say anything about it to <u>anyone</u>, and I didn't.

About a year later, I worked for Uncle Parker cleaning up the old cabin he lived in. Despite his disregard for some laws, he was good to me. He gave me my first watch and Coke money. There were always a lot of people at his cabin. I thought they were great people; however, looking back, I realize now that most of them were not so great.

One time a man named Will said he wanted to show me something in the field behind my uncle's cabin. The field was covered with ripening watermelons. Carefully hidden under each of those watermelons was a pint of illegal white lightning.

One day Uncle Parker asked if I wanted to make some money. He said he would give me a nickel for each empty whiskey bottle I could collect for him. I hit all the saloons in town and put every bottle I could find in a tow sack and kept them until Uncle Parker came by and picked them up. I had to promise him I would never say anything to my mother about what I was doing and I knew I better not.

I was making pretty good money at bottle collecting, so I decided to expand my business. I got two of my school buddies to start picking up bottles for me and I would give them three cents for each one.

I was doing really well as a supplier until my mother caught me. She found my most recently collected empty whiskey bottles in the coalhouse where I was hiding them. She smashed all of them, busted my butt, and banished her brother, Parker, from our house. She said he was not going to make a heathen out of me. It was a year or so before Mother relented and let Uncle Parker come around again. I had really missed him.

Uncle Parker later went to work as a cab company dispatcher. When I was about 14, he called Mother and asked if I could work some with the cab company delivering prescriptions for a pharmacy. I did that for a while until I found out that was just a front. I was actually making house calls to deliver moonshine. Burnt once, I didn't want anything to do with that. So that was the end of my career as a moonshiner's helper.

Still a youth, but now without my uncle's help, I worked several more jobs to help support our family. I worked at three homes where my job was to keep the coal furnaces loaded with coal for heat. I would stoke them at night and again from 6 to 7 a.m., and then refill the furnaces with coal. In the summers, I would take care of yards. In school, I would clean up the dining room in exchange for my lunch. From the age of 15 to 17, I worked for the schools when school was out doing painting, mowing, and washing windows.

In high school, I played football and basketball. I had grown to 6 feet, 5 inches tall, but only weighed 140 pounds. After one year in football, our coach said he wanted me to stick to basketball and practice year-round. My dad taught me that it took hard work—really hard work—to succeed in life. I had to try harder than the next guy. In Kentucky, basketball was everything. I made the first team in the ninth grade and became a pretty good player.

I left school in the 11th grade. To his credit, my coach tried his best to talk me out of doing that. He said he was working on a scholarship for me to go to the University of Kentucky. But I wanted to help my parents, and I had decided that going into the service was the best way to do it.

I came to Texas for the first time at 18 by way of the U. S. Air Force, taking my basic training at Lackland Air Force Base in San Antonio. My next stop was Bergstrom AFB in Austin. My salary was a meager $95 a month, but I immediately started sending $50 of it to my mother.

One of the first things I wanted to do after getting out of basic training was get my GED (high school equivalency diploma). A woman at the air base library helped me through the process. I took six tests and failed one of them, but my overall grade average was 78 and that was enough to pass. I was one proud airman with that diploma.

Ernie Hinkle

From 1951 to 1959, I served in the 27th Fighter Wing of the 808th Air Force and got to travel to Japan, England, Midway, Wake Island, and Guam. During that time, I made some life-long friends such as Pete Corbett, James Wood, Bill Boitnott, and many others.

After spending eight great years in the Air Force, I was a staff sergeant. But, my rank was frozen so I decided to leave the military and go into law enforcement. That turned out to be one of the best decisions I ever made.

Sgt. E. Hinkle, Hokkaido, Japan, 1953

THE ACADEMY

If at First You Don't Succeed...

It took me three tries and two and a half years to pass the Austin Police Department entrance exam. I took the first test while I was still in the Air Force and just kept trying until I succeeded.

Back then, the department didn't have a training academy building. Cadets met in the line-up room at police headquarters in the 700 block of East 7th Street.

The 23rd Cadet Class started Sept. 30, 1960 with 17 cadets. During our 17 weeks of training, we were in class from 8 a.m. to 5 p.m., Monday through Friday, and on Saturdays we had OJT (on-the-job training) riding with a commissioned officer or a sergeant detective.

During the week Lt. Pete Weaver taught most of our classes. And, one day a week, local long-time FBI Special Agent Ernie Kuhnel taught practical problems. Both men were excellent instructors and showed a lot of patience with the class.

During the first 30 minutes each day, we had a spelling test. My spelling was awful. In the first grade, I had trouble spelling my own name. I spent a lot of time learning to spell and kept a dictionary always with me.

One of my first street experiences happened while riding with my training officer, Jimmy Reed. We were running after a burglary suspect who had run from a building he had been hiding in. We were down on the lower end of Holly Street, east of downtown. I was hot on his trail when he just disappeared. At that moment, I fell into a swimming pool off Holly Street and landed on top of him. He could swim, but I couldn't. I hung on to him until we got to the edge of the pool where I got him out and cuffed him. The irony is that I really believe he saved me from drowning. I never did tell him I couldn't swim.

Back in class the next Monday morning we all exchanged stories from our weekend ride-along experiences. That's when we began to realize that this was going to be a job where we had to wear many hats. Our training would be extremely important.

Ernie Hinkle

Another thing I started to understand was that for the majority of time, the only contact most citizens had with the Police Department was when officers responded to calls. I developed an attitude of wanting to talk with people under different circumstances rather than just answering a call.

On another OJT night, November 3, 1960, I was assigned to ride with Sgt. Detective Robert Wisian, a hardworking, very professional officer. Wisian had received an "attempted suicide" call in the 2200 block of San Antonio Street, west of the University of Texas campus. When we arrived, we saw that it was an all-girls rooming house. The housemother told Wisian that a room at the top of the stairs was locked and that she could smell gas coming from the room.

We tried to force our way in, but that didn't work. Wisian told me to keep trying while he went downstairs to see if the housemother had a master key. As I worked to force the door open, the gas fumes were so overwhelming that I could hardly breathe. I kept desperately kicking at the door and finally the lock broke.

I found that someone had pushed a mattress against the door from inside. Without turning the light on, which might have ignited the gas fumes, I discovered a young woman under the mattress.

I picked her up and carried her limp body down the stairs and outside. I was gagging for fresh air. As we got outside, I heard her groan so I knew that she was still alive. The sergeant had already called for an ambulance and then he went back upstairs and turned the gas off. By the time the ambulance arrived, her life now saved, the young woman was crying and telling us that she was sorry for what she had tried to do.

Wisian found the suicide note she had written:

> What is this prying on my mind,
> An unrest which surmounts and remains.
> Oh God what can I do to find
> Peace of mind—I am going insane.
> Death seems to be the only way,

A complete darkness and stillness.
It will be the price I have to pay
To quieten the hell and let me rest.

Later, I learned she had recovered and seemed to be doing well. Thank goodness, her family never had to read that note she left.

We spent our last three weeks of training in the classroom taking tests and working practical problems, or at the pistol range taking firearms training. I was selected class president and felt very honored until I was told I had to speak at the graduation ceremony. The 23rd Cadet Class graduated on January 20, 1961. This was my speech, although it's hard to call it a speech since I was almost speechless when I gave it:

"Honorable Mayor Pro-Tem, City Council Members, City Manager…, Chief Miles, Honored Guests, Ladies and Gentlemen:

First, I would like to express my appreciation to members of my class for the honor they have given me to represent them here tonight. I feel fortunate in just being a member of this class. Having been elected as president means more to me than I know how to say. I will always do my very best to live up to the honor you have given me as president and will always be grateful.

We, the 23rd Cadet Class of the Austin Police Department, want to thank everyone concerned for the opportunity afforded us in becoming members of this class. We are proud in having been selected as prospective patrolmen and for the training we have received in the past seventeen weeks. We would like to thank Chief Miles for obtaining the excellent instructors from federal, state, county, and our own instructors, who have been so dedicated and worked so hard with us every day for the past seventeen weeks. We are indeed thankful to them for the understanding and consideration they have shown us during our training.

We feel we have had the best training possible to qualify us as police officers. Our training will help enable us to fulfill our obligation to the community, our chief, and the department. It is very hard to describe the training program. One would have to attend the training school to really understand and appreciate its value. Through our training, we have experienced some of the responsibilities of law enforcement officers and feel our fundamental duty is to serve mankind, to safeguard lives and property, and to respect the constitutional rights of all men to liberty, equality, and justice. Having chosen law enforcement as our profession, we will constantly strive to serve mankind and to be true to the ethics of police service.

This is more than just a job to us. It has been the desire of each and every one in this class to become a member of the Austin Police Department's team, to work with our fellow officers, and to serve our chief and the people of Austin to the best of our ability. We are proud in becoming members of one of the best police departments in our country, the Austin Police Department, for we are well aware of its creed and practices as to courtesy, honesty, personal integrity and, at all times, fair dealings. This, I must say in all sincerity, is not only advocated, but also carried out by those charged with its responsibility.

Thank you,
Ernest Hinkle, Jr."

23rd Cadet Class — Graduated January 20, 1961

Front Row: Lt Bill Purse, Capt B. H. Rosen, Chief R. A. Miles, Deputy Chief R. B. Laws, Lt W. S. "Pete" Weaver.

Middle Row: D. Roper, D. Hicks, J. Palmer, R. Givens, E. Hinkle, Ramiro Martinez, W. Tayle, D. McCullough.

Back Row: W. Phillips, R. Politvitz, J. Leo, R. Willhoite, S. Ferris, A. Riley, L. Jones, D. Woodall, C. Lange.

ROOKIE YEAR

First Assignment

My first assignment was a walking beat in downtown Austin. I would be working with two other officers: Mark Cutler, who was the senior officer, and Don Carpenter. My intersection was 6th Street and Congress Avenue – the heart of the city – from 11 a.m. to 1 p.m. and from 4-6 p.m.

Each day at those times, we had to be in the intersection directing traffic and pedestrians, which was an okay job. When not working traffic, we walked the streets and alleys, met a lot of the people who worked in the stores along the avenue, and kept the transients moving.

Back then, we didn't have portable radios, so once every hour we had to go to a red call box in the 100 block of West 6th Street to contact the dispatcher. When we made an arrest, that was the procedure we used to get a police car to come by and pick up the person to take them to jail. But sometimes it was extremely difficult to get an unwilling drunk to accompany me to the red call box.

Lady to Officer: "Kiss My Butt"

Being senior officer, Cutler kept us busy checking the alleys, keeping the traffic moving, writing parking tickets, and so forth. A big man with big ears, Cutler worked hard, had a rough voice, and seemed like a tough guy. But he had a tender heart and was like a big teddy bear when you got to know him.

Drivers were always trying to double-park their vehicles along Congress Avenue in the 500, 600, and 700 blocks. It seemed like Cutler was constantly blowing his whistle and pointing at a vehicle to get the driver to move along.

One afternoon, a woman double-parked in the 600 block to pick up some dry cleaning. Cutler started with his whistle, indicating with his hand for her to move. When she ignored him, he walked briskly toward her car, telling her that she was blocking traffic and needed to move. I was following him. With

[15]

the lady still not budging, he stuck his head in the window and loudly blew his whistle. Then he yelled, "Move it!"

She looked at him and yelled, "Kiss my ass!" I was standing behind Cutler and said to her, "Ma'am, he will! But first, please pull around the corner on 7th Street and he'll go over there." At that, she drove off, burning rubber. I don't know who Cutler was most angry with, me for spouting off to a citizen, or that lady. But as soon as he cooled off, we both had a good laugh about it.

A Two-by-Four?

Most often, the walking beat involved routine traffic and pedestrian control; however, as with all police work, things are never routine all the time. You never know what the next call will be.

In the 1960s, the Greyhound Bus Station was at the northeast corner of 4th Street and Congress. I got to know the folks who worked there by stopping by on my walking rounds.

One day the ticket agent told me a man had been in the men's restroom for about three hours and asked if I would check on him. I went into the restroom and, looking over the stall, I saw a man sitting on the commode. I knocked on the door and asked if he was okay. He said, "God, no!" Looking over the top of the stall again, I asked if I could help him. Since I'm tall, I could easily see him. He told me that he had a two-by-four up his butt and couldn't get it out. (A two-by-four is a piece of lumber, about 2 inches by 4 inches, and comes from a lumberyard about eight feet long.)

I felt certain that he was a mental case and decided that I would simply try to talk him out of the stall. I told him I was a police officer and wanted to help him. He asked if I could get a saw. I told him I would go get one.

I went back to the ticket agent and asked him to call the Police Department to send a police car and a backup to the bus station. Then, I went back to the restroom and told the still-sitting man that I was back with a saw and I would be coming into the stall. I asked him to cover his eyes.

I went into the stall and pretended to saw the two-by-four, then helped him stand up. I put the handcuffs on him and walked him out to the waiting police car. He thanked me very much. Another officer took him to the State Hospital.

I don't know if I handled that right, but I didn't have to fight him and he was happy to shed that two-by-four, even if it was only in his mind.

Small Event Incites a Big Ruckus

After I adjusted to the walking beat, I liked directing traffic and the contact with people. The two officers I worked with, Cutler and Carpenter, were very good cops and I learned a lot from them.

One Friday afternoon traffic was particularly heavy. Suddenly, I noticed what looked like a disturbance at 7th and Congress. Hurrying in that direction, I saw an older woman chasing a man around two vehicles. About the time I got there, the man jumped into the front car and locked the doors. Then, the woman began angrily banging on his car window with her purse. I tried to calm her down but had little success. However, I was able to determine that there had been a minor collision between the two cars, front-end to rear-end. We were in front of the Stephen F. Austin Hotel and a crowd began to gather.

The woman told me she was the wife of a very prominent Texas businessman and that the "fool" in the car in front of her had backed into her car. However, a witness contradicted her version saying that the car in the back had bumped the car in the front. During the incident, the man driving the front car got out asking her to give him her name. She told him to just get out of her way and then they started arguing loudly. At that point, the man jumped back into his car.

I told the woman that it was only a minor collision and I would make an information report for both parties and then we could all leave. She apparently didn't like hearing that and started telling me "where I could go."

In those days, we wore a shoulder strap on our Sam Browns (a leather belt and holster for our handgun and equipment). Obviously still very angry, the woman grabbed me by the strap and began pulling me around the cars. It wasn't painful, but it was beginning to get on my nerves.

I managed to break free of her grip and was trying to retreat from the cars when the driver of the front car, body shop owner Dude Stelfox, rolled down his car window and called out, "Officer, get in here."

I opened the door and jumped into his car. About that time, the woman's son came up and got his mother under control.

I got the information I needed and gave it to each driver. Stelfox told me that he stopped his car when her car hit his car from behind. He spotted a new dent in his bumper and so asked for her name. That was when the "you know what" hit the fan.

I was sure glad to see her son. I didn't know how I was going to get away from there without cuffing and arresting the woman, and I really didn't want to do that.

Public Intoxication

That same day, I was directing traffic at 6th and Congress. A man ran up to me and said that a fellow in a bar in the 100 block of East 6th was throwing beer bottles and wanting to fight. I went over there with no back up or any way to call in. The man in question was in his forties, well dressed, and well lubricated.

"I am ready to kick your butt," he warned as I walked into the bar.

When I told him I didn't want to fight him, he said, "Take that gun off and let's get it on." I said I would just as soon shoot him than take my gun off. Then I told him to shut up, turn around, and get against the wall.

Thank God, that's what he did. I cuffed him, took him to the call box, and requested a unit to come pick him up. He got booked for disturbance and public intoxication.

Patrol Platoon

It took me a while to get used to the unpredictable weather and being on my feet all day, but I found the walking beat to be good duty. However, I wanted to do even more as a police officer. After six months, I passed my probationary period and got assigned to Capt. Wilfred Swinney's platoon.

In the 1960s, APD had three patrol platoons. The schedules were from 7 a.m. to 3 p.m., 3 p.m. to 11 p.m., and 11 p.m. to 7 a.m. At that time the department divided the city into four sectors: Adam (North Austin); Baker (Central Austin); Charlie (the UT area east of IH-35 and south to the city limits); and, David (Southwest Austin). The department only had its downtown headquarters, no substations.

Austin was much smaller and quite different in those days. We didn't have a narcotics problem and the public seemed more police-friendly than today.

In Capt. Swinney's platoon, I started on the evening shift working Baker Sector. This was a busy district that included downtown, Brackenridge Hospital and the UT area west of IH-35.

I spent a lot of time at the Brackenridge emergency room investigating all injuries that came in due to wrecks, assaults, fights, and child abuse. Quite often, I had to arrest drunks causing problems at the hospital.

I met one of my life-long friends at the ER, Dr. Bud Dryden. He was the trauma physician and seemed to be there all the time. He was a down-to-earth guy, very straightforward, and a great doctor. I witnessed him stitch up a knife-fight victim and then deliver a baby behind the next curtained-off stall, going from one patient to another. A lot of people he never even charged. I would hear him say, "You can pay me when you have the money."

Ernie Hinkle

When not at the ER, I was driving Baker 1 (my assigned car unit)–a 1957 Dodge painted a solid pinkish-salmon color. It had no emergency lights, and only a one-way police radio. To stop a vehicle, I had to use a hand-held red spotlight. Also, the car had an interesting hole in the floorboard below the gas pedal. This hole was caused when an officer was checking the safety on his 12-gauge shotgun. Apparently, it wasn't on safety. I had to have a carpet business custom-cut a piece of carpet to fit the floorboard to cover up the hole.

Rescuing an 18-Month-Old Toddler Locked in a Bathroom

I received an "assist complainant" call to a house on Enfield Road. When I got there, an obviously distressed woman met me saying her 18-month-old boy was locked in their bathroom and she couldn't get him out. I checked the door and saw that the hinges were unfortunately on the inside.

Meanwhile, I could hear the little boy crying. The frantic mother wanted me to break the door down, but I didn't want to damage any property, so I asked if the bathroom had a window. She took me outside and I saw that the window was open. I told her I could go through the window and open the bathroom door from the inside. I pulled my car up to the window and got on top so I could climb through.

As I was letting myself down, I stepped on the bathtub soap holder. Turns out it wasn't designed to support 6-foot-5 cops. It gave way, I fell into the bathtub and the tile from the wall above the tub crashed down on top of me.

I got myself up and picked up the little boy who was now really crying. I opened the bathroom door and handed the terrified child to his frazzled mother.

Unfortunately, the bathroom was one big mess. I told the lady I was so sorry that I hadn't intended for that to happen.

"Wouldn't it have been better to just break the door down?" she asked. I told her again that I was sorry, gave her the phone number for the city's legal department, and got myself out of there.

Thirty-Three Minutes of Freedom

I was on patrol downtown when Sgt. John Pope broadcast a report of a purse snatching at the Commodore Perry Hotel. He gave the description of a man with a striped brown shirt, about six feet tall, 150 pounds, in his mid-20s. I checked the streets east of the location and stopped in an alley off the 1000 block of Trinity Street.

Almost immediately, I saw a man matching the description walking fast and going north on Trinity. When I stopped him, I could tell he had been running, but he was wearing a white shirt instead of a striped shirt. He identified himself and said he was a soldier attached to a missile unit. Sgt. Pope took him back to the hotel and got him identified as the person who had grabbed some woman's purse. He had $2.87 on him when arrested.

While Sgt. Pope dealt with the suspect, I checked the trash bins. Luckily, I found his brown and white-striped shirt hidden in the dumpster at St. Mary's School just east of the Commodore Perry.

Later, I learned that earlier that day, at 11 a.m., the man had been before a judge for auto theft. He had entered a plea of guilty and received a two-year probationary sentence. Unreformed, at 11:33 a.m., he had been arrested for the purse snatching. The judge soon revoked his probation and the guy went to prison. The soldier had enjoyed only 33 minutes of freedom between the time he left court and his arrest on a new charge.

Saxophones Found, But No Players

Shortly after midnight one night, while patrolling downtown Austin, I happened to see six saxophones on the steps of

[21]

the Texas Supreme Court Building, still in their instrument cases. Unable to find players for them, I started checking schools. I discovered that the door at Pearce Junior High School's band room was unlocked and open. I thought I had solved the mystery, but it was later determined that the musical instruments had not come from Pearce, and no one at the Supreme Court played the saxophone. We never did find where they had come from.

A Pony in a Falcon

I got a call to investigate a collision at the corner of 3rd and Nueces Streets. When I arrived, I was surprised to see a Shetland pony in the back seat of a Ford Falcon. The driver of the car had backed into a parked vehicle. My partner, Officer Albert Riley, came by to help direct traffic.

After piecing the facts together, I determined that the pony's owner had been taking it to Oak Hill in the back of his Ford Falcon and had stopped at a feed store. When he got back into his car, the Ford wouldn't start. He got a ride home, got another car and came back, but he decided to try again to start the Falcon. He was successful this time and, in backing up, he bumped into his other car.

The owner of the cars was a friendly guy, but drunk. We arrested him for public intoxication, impounded both of his vehicles and put the pony to pasture at the city lot. The driver wanted to ride the pony to Oak Hill, but I reminded him that he didn't have a saddle. At that, he started laughing and said, "I'm too drunk to ride that damn horse anyway."

The Officer, the Drunk, and the Monkey

One day in August 1961, I was on patrol in the 500 block of East 6th when I saw a man standing in the street holding a spider monkey. He was cursing at passing traffic and generally creating a disturbance.

I stopped and walked over to him. I told him to get back on the sidewalk and move along. He said, "Okay," and walked over to the sidewalk. But when I got in my car to drive off, I saw that he had gone back in the street again.

"This monkey will eat you up," the man threatened as I arrested him for public intoxication and being in the roadway.

Back then, our police cars were not air-conditioned, had no seat belts, and no screen between the front and back seats to protect us from people we arrested while we transported them to jail. I put the man and his monkey in the right front seat.

As I started off, he flung the monkey in my face to keep me occupied while he jumped out of the car. The darn monkey began biting my ear and screaming. I finally knocked the nasty-tempered little animal off me and it jumped out the car window.

I ran after the drunk, re-arrested him, and then caught his monkey.

I cuffed the drunk, got him back in the car and tried to find something to tie up the monkey with. I needed my belt, so I couldn't use that. I thought about putting the monkey in the trunk, but was afraid it might suffocate or die from the heat. Meanwhile, the monkey was raising hell just looking at me. He clearly didn't like police officers. After finally getting both man and monkey calmed down enough to sit in the car, I again started driving toward the police station.

This time, I made it only about a half block when again the drunk threw the monkey on me and bailed again.

After being the victim in this not-so-funny-to-me comedy routine three times, I finally called for an officer to assist me. The call went out as, "Assist officer with a drunk monkey!"

Officer Ted Hargis came to my rescue and took the monkey to the Humane Society while I took care of the drunk.

As word of the incident got around, I had to put up with a lot of friendly kidding. I just about lost my cool the last time the drunk threw that monkey on me. I came very close to using "necessary force" to knock the crap out of that monkey–very close!

First Homicide

I received a call to investigate a disturbance in the 1200 block of West 12th at the Maroon Grill Sandwich Shop. That was just around the corner from what was then Austin High School. I arrived about 1:45 p.m. as several people ran from the scene. I saw a crowd of students in front of the grill and a young man lying on the sidewalk in a pool of blood. He was transported to Brackenridge Hospital ER and died about 1 a.m. the next day.

At the scene, I talked to a group of students who told me the 17-year-old student had gone to the grill for lunch. They said that a car drove up and several men got out and started a fight with the teenager. He fell to the ground and they ran off. I asked four of the witnesses if they could identify the persons involved in the fight and they said they would try. At the high school, we got a yearbook and the witnesses were able to identify the person who had the knife. After the fight, the assailants had run from the car, so I had it impounded.

Based on the witnesses' statements and the yearbook identification, Justice of the Peace Bob Kuhn issued a murder with malice warrant against 17-year-old Victor Ontiveros. Other officers arrested him the next day.

I did nothing special in this case. I simply responded to a call, but felt we owed the victim justice. It bothered me that the fight hadn't somehow been prevented. This first homicide of my career helped me realize just how special life is and how quickly it can be taken away.

Rookie of the Year

At the end of my first 18 months with the department, I was invited to attend the Austin Citizens Safety Council's Second Annual Police Awards Banquet at Municipal Auditorium on Nov. 28, 1962. The guest speaker was George Beto, Director of the Texas Department of Corrections. The Outstanding Officer of the Year was Sgt. Bert Bowman; Sgt. Fred Hooper was Outstanding Sgt. Investigator of the Year; Officer Mark Cutler was Outstanding Traffic Officer of the Year; and to my surprise, Ernie Hinkle was Rookie Officer of the Year. I didn't think I had done anything particularly outstanding and could think of other officers who should have gotten the award. In fact, right up until they read my name, I thought I was just there for a free meal.

Clayton E. Evans with the Junior Chamber of Commerce presented me with a beautiful gold watch. I felt very honored.

What's Next?

At the end of my rookie year, I thought I would transfer to the motorcycle patrol. I had never been on a motorcycle, but I had a young family and the motorcycle unit worked during the daytime. Motor officers also got more overtime.

I had been making $500 a month in the Air Force before I got hired by APD. When I started in the cadet class, my monthly salary dropped to $310. After my probationary period, I got a $10 raise. Of course, I had known what the salary would be before I started with the department. Still, it was a tight squeeze to support my family.

I talked to Sgt. Jack Irwin and newly promoted Sgt. Mark Cutler about transferring to Motors, as they called the unit. They supervised the unit and taught me how to operate a motorcycle. Sgt. Irwin even drove me to the Department of Public Safety to get a motorcycle operator license. The DPS examiner gave me the written test and I passed it. Now came the driving part. The examiner rode in a police unit with Sgt. Irwin behind me as I rode the motorcycle.

"When the horn sounds once, turn right–when it sounds two times, turn left," the examiner told me. We started down Denson Drive from the DPS driver's license office. The horn sounded once and I turned right into a private driveway. The car stopped. "Hinkle, you big dummy," the examiner said. "You are supposed to stay on public property." He then told me to meet him back at the office. It embarrassed me—I knew I had screwed up—but I had just been following instructions.

I got back to the office, met Sgt. Irwin and he handed me my license, which back then was just a small piece of paper. We had a good laugh about it and I went in and thanked the trooper, who told me a story that happened just the day before. He was giving an exam riding in a car with a lady. When they got to the intersection of Lamar Boulevard and Denson, he told her to turn left. She did—right into oncoming traffic. A car hit them on the passenger side, but luckily, no one was hurt. Not surprisingly, she failed her test.

MOTORS

Traffic Division

Motorcycle Shift - 1963 - In Front of U.T. Tower

Within a month after getting my motorcycle license, I transferred to the Traffic Division's Motorcycle Unit. In the 1960s and 1970s, APD used three-wheel Harley Davidsons. The department had no two-wheelers. That's because Chief Miles thought two-wheelers were too dangerous.

I was assigned to Sgt. Irwin's shift working 7 a.m. to 6 p.m. with a one-hour break for dinner. There were 12 officers on my shift, a dedicated group who worked hard but had fun.

My district was the downtown area, which I knew well after having been assigned the business district walking beat. In the 200 block on the east side of Congress were several bars, pool halls, and beer joints. I was riding through the east alley in that block when I saw a drunk cursing and mad because he had been kicked out of one of the bars. I arrested him for public intoxication, sat him on the back of my motorcycle, and handcuffed him to the handles on the motor. I called the dispatcher to inform him that Motor 361 was en route to jail with a drunk and took off toward headquarters. When I pulled up at the back of the police station where we unloaded prisoners, the sergeant met me along with several other officers.

"Ernie, what do you have?" my sergeant asked. He didn't allow any time for me to answer before he offered some blunt coaching: "You don't transport prisoners on the motors—you call for a car. Do you understand?"

"Yes sir," I said.

"You might as well let him go now," the sergeant said after taking another look at my prisoner. "Looks like that ride sobered him up." I let him go. He did seem a lot more sober and I was better educated.

I guess I didn't realize it when I asked for the transfer to Motors, but 90 percent of the unit's responsibility was traffic enforcement. Our sergeant expected us to write plenty of tickets even though he said he would rather let a close violation go rather than us issuing a citation. I never was a big-ticket writer. It had to be an intersection-to-intersection infraction before I would stop a car. But there were still plenty of hazardous violations out there.

We also did a lot of traffic control. The State Highway Department was building IH-35 in the early 1960s and I escorted many trucks carrying long concrete beams for overpass construction. Our unit also was responsible for funeral escorts, timed parking zones, tow-away zones, parades, radar speed enforcement and assorted other duties.

When we worked radar, we would team up with a partner. Some of my partners were Bill Landis, Delbert McCullough, Albert Riley, Justin Schaffer, Alvin DeVane and Harry Eastman. We worked a lot of radar. Each team would issue about 20 speeding or no driver's license citations, and 10-15 warning tickets a day.

To stay busy, I volunteered to take funeral escorts, sometimes three or four a day, which took up three or four hours. Back then, the city did not charge for this service. I still have a drawer full of letters from people thanking me for escorting their family members' funerals. These days funeral escorts are handled by off-duty officers and the families are charged.

I had some mighty cold and rainy escorts. The department didn't furnish winter clothes to motorcycle officers–just a light Ike Jacket and a police cap. We weren't even issued helmets until late 1969. To keep warm, I would wrap my legs with newspaper pages, using rubber bands to keep them in place. I finally bought a leather jacket for $40 at Academy Surplus on West 6th Street. I paid $20 down and $10 for the next two months. That jacket made a big difference.

Attempted Suicide in Zilker Park

We had to qualify with our sidearm every month. Back then, the pistol range was just off Barton Springs Road on Delaney Street next to Zilker Park, only a short distance from downtown.

I was on my way to qualify one day when I noticed a car parked off the roadway under some trees in the park. I didn't think much about it but, after I finished shooting, I went back the same way and noticed the car was still there. Stopping to check, I saw a hose in the tailpipe going through the trunk of the car. The car was running, had fogged up inside and the driver was slumped over the wheel. I broke out the window with my pistol and pulled a man out of the car. I pushed on his chest and administered mouth-to-mouth resuscitation until I finally heard him groan. Then I called for an ambulance. He was rushed to Brackenridge Hospital, where he recovered.

Snowball Fight

During one of the first snows we had in Austin after I joined the motorcycle unit, Albert Riley and I were working the UT area. As we drove down San Antonio Street, we started taking on snowballs. The girls at one of the sorority houses were having a snowball fight and we were handy targets. To the girls' surprise, Albert and I both came off our motors and started throwing snowballs back at them. The battle lasted until we started getting the worst of it, so we decided to get ourselves out of there.

Someone must have seen the fight while failing to see the humor in it. However it happened, Chief Miles got wind of it. He asked us how it happened and whether we didn't have more important things to do. But we could tell it was all he could do to keep from laughing.

Escorting Carol Burnett

I got a call from Sgt. Cutler to help with an escort. He said the TV star, Carol Burnett, was coming to Austin and that City Councilman Bob Armstrong would be picking her up at the airport. The city was going to rename Congress Avenue Carol Burnett Avenue for the day and we were to escort them to 11th Street and Congress for the ceremony.

Our route-to-be was west on Manor Road from the airport to West Frontage Road, south to 11th Street, and west to Congress Avenue. The escort was going without a hitch until we got to 10th Street at East Frontage Road. For some reason, Sgt. Cutler turned right at 10th Street and I went on to 11th. I looked back and saw that the councilman must have tried to follow both of us. In his confusion, he hit the curb at 10th and East Frontage Road and knocked off a hubcap. I turned back, helped him get off the curb, found his hubcap, got him on the roadway, and asked him to follow me. "Hinkle," he said, "I know the way from here and I don't need any more help."

Seven-Fingered Jack

I got assigned to close-patrol a Safeway grocery store in the 1100 block of IH-35 Frontage Road because the store was experiencing a lot of shoplifting during the daytime. As time would permit, I would drive by the store. On one shift, I noticed a man acting suspiciously in front of the store and rode my motorcycle up to him.

As I got off the motor, he took off running. I chased him to 11th Street and then east on 11th. He was about a half block ahead of me. He slowed down whenever I got close, and then he would take off again. When we approached Rosewood Street, he held out his left arm and gave a signal that he was turning left. As I rounded the corner at 11th and Rosewood, he stood about a block ahead of me motioning for me to come on. I knew then the chase was over. The guy was either real fast or I was real slow.

Hot and sweaty, I made it back to my motorcycle and called in what had happened. Sgt. Sam Smith came by. The sergeant asked what was going on and I told him. Then he started laughing. He said I had been after a character called Seven-Fingered Jack, and that he had baited me into chasing him.

Turns out that Seven-Fingered Jack would try all new officers. He had out-run most all of them. The older officers would keep Jack's little game a secret until someone chased him again. I saw him several times after that. He would always smile, wave, and act like he was going to run.

I never learned how Seven-Fingered Jack got his name, but I did learn something from Sgt. Smith: It's not against the law to run.

A Cheap Traffic Ticket

One day at Show-up, a fellow officer – I won't use his name for reasons that will soon be obvious – told me that anytime I needed to write a ticket to look for Roy's Cab No. 8. The driver (whose last name was Howard), had only one arm.

I didn't think much about it then, but as what that officer said began to soak in, it began to make me angry. That's not how a professional law enforcement officer should conduct his business. It's all about service to the public, not easy tickets.

As time permitted, I would look for the cab, but for another reason. I finally spotted him and pulled him over in the 1400 block of East 12th Street. When I asked for his driver's license, he said, "Officer, I don't have one. And if I get another ticket, I can't drive the cab anymore." I asked him why he didn't have a license and he told me he couldn't pass the test. I told him I wasn't going to give him a ticket, but that I would like to help him get his license. Hearing that, he got tears in his eyes.

I got a DPS Driver's License handbook for him to study and then went to the DPS driver's license office to talk with a sergeant I knew there. The state officer helped me set it up to give Howard an oral driver's test. Within a month, I went with Howard so he could take his exam. He passed both the oral and driving tests and we left there with his driver's license. I don't know who was happier, Mr. Howard or me.

I took great pleasure in telling the easy-ticket officer that the driver of Roy's Taxi No. 8 now had a driver's license. I was also glad when that officer later resigned from law enforcement. I had no respect for him.

Meeting President Kennedy

On Nov. 22, 1963, our motorcycle shift had been assigned to go to Bergstrom Air Force Base to meet the Secret Service for escort duty. President John F. Kennedy would be coming to Austin from Dallas and we were to escort his motorcade. The Secret Service told us he would be departing Love Field in Dallas at 2:35 p.m. and arriving at Bergstrom AFB in Austin at 3:15 p.m. We were to escort the motor caravan to the Commodore Perry Hotel to arrive there at 3:55 p.m. Then we were to continue the escort to the Governor's Mansion in Austin arriving at 6:00 p.m.

I was headed down Airport Boulevard on the way to Bergstrom AFB when a car came up beside me and the driver motioned me to pull over. He asked me if I had heard that President Kennedy had just been shot. Of course, I had not. I sat in his car for a while and listened to the news on the radio. The assassination stunned and saddened everyone, including my fellow officers.

So Glad to See My Partner

I was working radar on Duval Street when a Yellow Cab drove up. The cabbie told me he had been driving his fare, a female, around for two hours. He said she didn't seem to know where she wanted to go. Worse than that, she had defecated in his cab, and the smell was really bad. My partner, Bill Landis, drove up and I told him what was going on. Meanwhile, I checked with our dispatcher and learned that the female rider had walked off from the Austin State Hospital on North Lamar.

Bill asked the cab driver what her fare was. He said she had already paid him $4 but owed him another $2. Bill asked him what the fare would be to the State Hospital, which the cabbie said would be another $1. Bill gave the driver $3 and told him to take her back to the State Hospital.

Black Cat

While checking tow-away zones on 19th Street (now MLK Boulevard) about 5 p.m. one day, I noticed that traffic seemed unusually heavy. I was at 19th and Lamar Boulevard when I heard horns blowing and tires squealing. I looked up 19th Street and saw an older model car backing up fast against oncoming traffic. Other motorists were trying to avoid the vehicle as the driver caused several near-collisions.

When I got him stopped, I saw that the back seat of his car had been taken out to make room for two barrels filled with slop. He said he picked the slop up every day at restaurants for his hogs. But I hadn't pulled him over to talk about hog slop. I asked him why he had been backing up and he offered what he seemed to think was a perfectly logical explanation.

"Look what happened to me already," he said. "The cops have got me! What would have happened if I had kept going when that black cat ran in front of me? If I had kept going, no telling what would have happened."

Before I could say anything, he offered me a piece of advice:

"Never go ahead when a black cat crosses your path."

I checked his driver's license and it was good. He said he was going another way just in case that black cat showed up again. I told him I was going another way, too, and let him go.

Excuses

No policeman wears a badge very long before he figures he's "heard them all."

Mike Cox, then police reporter for the Austin American-Statesman, asked me one day what excuses I had been given by people trying to get out of tickets. Mike knew I wasn't a big-ticket writer, but I had heard plenty of excuses.

While working the UT area, I was going north in the 2100 block of Guadalupe when a sports car passed me southbound going fast. I turned around and took after him. The car went through a red light at 19th Street and Guadalupe, went south on Guadalupe, and stopped at the Southwestern Bell Telephone building in the 1500 block. I pulled up behind him.

The driver got out of his car and started walking toward the door of the building. "Hey, wait a minute," I said. "I didn't get a clock on you, but I saw you go through the red light." He said, very impatiently, "Officer, I don't have time to talk about it now. I've got to get these birth control pills to my girlfriend." I told him to go ahead and I would wait for him. I didn't want to interfere with his personal life. When he returned, I gave him a red light ticket and marked "court case" on it. I wanted the judge to hear his reason.

People stopped for driving recklessly usually say they're late for work, have to go the bathroom, were about to run out of gas, had left their glasses at home or dropped a cigarette between their legs.

Motorists stopped for driving while intoxicated all seemed to claim they'd had only two beers or two drinks.

Mike was a great reporter and wrote some good stories. Seems like he was always at the police station and was on top of what was going on. He was later the spokesman for the Department of Public Safety and the Texas Rangers. Mike became a good friend and I wasn't afraid to tell him anything.

A Learning Experience

One morning I was going to a traffic assignment at Manor Road and the East Frontage Road of IH-35. About 7 a.m., I came up behind a new Ford sedan going really slow. Then the vehicle started swerving all over the roadway. Finally, it hit the curb and stopped.

The male driver could barely stand up and had an odor of an alcoholic beverage. I couldn't get much information out of him because he was too drunk. I called for a patrol car, arrested him for DWI and had his car impounded.

In 1963, the police pound was on 8th Street just across from the station. The procedure on DWI was that after the suspect was booked into jail, the warrant officer would take them before the municipal judge. The judge would either release them on bond or transfer them to the Travis County Jail.

As I was leaving the station around 5:30 p.m. that evening, I happened to notice the DWI subject's vehicle was still on the impound lot. That seemed strange, so I circled back, went up to the jail, and asked Lt. Jake Barnett if the DWI I had arrested that morning was still there. The lieutenant said the man was still too drunk to take before the judge.

We talked it over and decided to check on him. When we looked in his cell, we saw that he could hardly sit up even though it had been hours since I had arrested him. We called for an ambulance and got him to Brackenridge Hospital ER where the doctor said he was a diabetic in bad condition. He was in the hospital about three days. The doctor told me he would not have lived another day without treatment. He also told me that a diabetic experiencing low blood sugar can appear to be drunk and even have an odor that smells like alcohol.

Driving While Intoxicated Arrest

I was working overtime one Saturday to beef-up the night patrol which was short on personnel. I was just leaving the station about 11 p.m. when a car in front of me went through a red light at a slow speed. I tried to stop the vehicle, but it kept going for several blocks, very slowly, before it finally stopped.

When I approached, I saw the driver was a female holding a drink. She started crying when she got out of the car. When she failed the field sobriety test, I arrested her for DWI and took her to Brackenridge Hospital for a blood test. This was in 1962 long before Intoxilyzer tests.

Sgt. Don Doyle met me at the hospital and we both heard her story. She was drunk, but clearly a nice person. She told us that she and her husband were from San Antonio and in Austin for a convention. She said they had an argument, he got out of the car, and that she had been driving around looking for him.

After getting her blood sample, I took her to jail. She wanted me to stay with her. I told her that I couldn't do that, but assured her she would be okay and would be seeing a judge in about five hours. She also asked if I could contact her husband, which was something I could do for her.

She said they were staying at the Holiday Inn on North IH-35. When I went back on the street about 1:30 a.m., I went to the hotel. Her husband had not made it back to their room, so I left information with the desk clerk on where he could find his wife and added that he could contact me if he needed more information.

I thought that was that, but about two months later, I received the following letter from the woman I had arrested:

March 22, 1962

Mr. Ernest Hinkle, 317

Dear Sir:

Thank you for your time and kindness in trying to contact my husband and for leaving the "message" with the clerk at the Holiday Inn.

I wish to tell you I appreciated your courtesy to me. You impressed me as being a very conscientious policeman doing his job well.

The outcome of my blood test was good, I am happy to say. The experience was bad as well as costly.

The trial was yesterday. My husband and I thought we should wait until then to say,

Thank you,
Signed . . .

Traffic Stop–Montopolis Bridge

About 2 o'clock one cold and rainy morning, I stopped an eastbound 1956 Ford sedan around the 2500 block of East 7th Street. I asked the driver, a man in his late 50s, to sit in my unit so we could be out of the weather. I frisked him and then he got in my unit.

He was very nice and said he had just gotten off work and was going home on Montopolis Drive. As I was writing a traffic ticket, I could tell he had been drinking and was a borderline DWI. Like they all say, he told me he'd had two beers after he got off work. I warned him about drinking and driving and then let him go.

A little later, I got a call to investigate a collision on the Montopolis Bridge. When I arrived, I saw the vehicle I had stopped earlier. As was common on that narrow bridge, the car had hit the guardrail and overturned. The driver I had lectured about drinking and driving got banged up pretty bad in the crash and spent several weeks in the hospital.

That was a good lesson for me and, hopefully, for him. From that day on, if I thought a driver had too much to drink, I would put them through the sobriety test. If they were borderline drunk, I would talk them into getting a cab or another driver. If they failed the test, they went to jail.

Routine Traffic Stop–Another Good Lesson

Working the streets, it's easy to let your guard down. I learned the hard way that when that happens, an officer puts himself in a bad situation. Eighty to eighty-five percent of the people police officers deal with are good, law-abiding citizens–sometimes they just make mistakes. The other fifteen to twenty percent are the problem. Unfortunately, at first you never know which group you are dealing with.

One time taking a situation for granted nearly got me hurt or killed. I was sitting in the 200 block of IH-35 northbound about 11:30 p.m. when a sedan passed me at a high rate of speed. I chased him at about 80 mph and got a good clock on the car. Then it slowed down.

I could see only one person in the vehicle. He took the 15th Street exit and finally stopped around the 1600 block of East Frontage Road. I called in the license number and location before I approached the car.

The driver was a well-dressed man. He was very nice and said he was sorry, that his speed just got away from him. I took his driver's license, and went to my unit to get a 10-55 (check for warrant and wanted information). I also wanted to check his car so I asked him to get out of the vehicle and sit in the front seat of my unit. I looked over the vehicle, which seemed okay. I walked back to my unit and told the man he was getting a speeding ticket for going 80 in a 55 mph zone.

Just as I was about to finish writing the ticket, the passenger door to my unit flew open and the man went down on the pavement. That's when I heard Officer Harry Eastman say, "Drop the knife if you want to live." About that time, the dispatcher called me asking if the subject was in custody. I advised that yes, he was, and that Officer Eastman had backed me up. The dispatcher then said the subject was wanted. The FBI had just identified him as the robber of several banks in the San Antonio area.

I hadn't paid any attention, but the man had his left arm lying across the bench seat in my unit. When Eastman came up on the right side of my unit, he saw the man had a Bowie knife in his hand and yanked him out of my unit.

On the way to the station, I asked the man if he would have stabbed me. He said if I had given him a ticket and let him go, nothing would have happened. On the other hand, he said if I had found out he was wanted by the FBI, he would have killed me to keep from going to jail – or tried.

That incident taught me a lesson that stuck with me for the rest of my career. From then on, I always made sure that I knew where a person's hands were when I dealt with them. I could never thank Eastman enough and I would always, time permitting, check on other officers who were working traffic stops. Eastman left APD and went to work at the UT Police Department as assistant chief. He died in 2004. He was a fine man, and a great officer.

Ernie Hinkle

Escorting Vice President Lyndon Baines Johnson

In 1962, whenever Vice President Lyndon Johnson came to Austin, the motorcycle platoon would assist the Secret Service in escorting him. Being from the Hill Country, Johnson came home as often as he could. Almost as frequently, he would change his destination at the last minute. This created a problem because the new route had not been checked out.

One time we were headed for Bergstrom Air Force Base when the Vice President decided he wanted to get a haircut. We escorted him to a barbershop in the west alley of the 500 block of Congress Avenue where he got his ears lowered. After that, he started walking around downtown and one of the Secret Service agents asked me to walk with them.

First, Johnson strolled over to Joseph's Men's Wear Shop in the 600 block of Congress on the east side. When he left there, he went north to Brazos Street toward the Driskill Hotel. Along this route, he came over to me, shook my hand, and said, "Officer, tell your chief he has a great police department and I appreciate the service you do for me." He started to leave, then turned around and asked, "Officer, what is your name?" It scared the heck out of me. He was really polite, but spoke in straightforward language. I responded, "Ernie Hinkle, sir." He then handed me a pass to the Vice President's Gallery in the U.S. Senate Chamber and said, "When you come to Washington, come see me and I'll take care of you." I never took him up on it, but I still have the card, just in case.

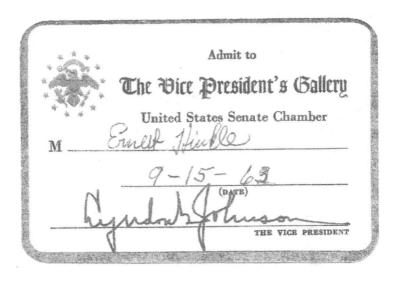

Admit to

The Vice President's Gallery

United States Senate Chamber

M _Ernest Hinkle_

_9-15-63_
(DATE)

Lyndon B. Johnson

THE VICE PRESIDENT

Escorting President Lyndon Baines Johnson

After President Kennedy was assassinated in 1963 and Johnson became President, he continued to visit Texas as often as he could. His ranch near Johnson City became known as "The Little White House." When he came through Austin, the motorcycle platoon would be assigned to escort him.

With safety now much tighter, we always took our directions from the Secret Service. Our routes would be changed or given to us only shortly before his arrival. If the weather was bad and the President's plane couldn't fly, we would escort Johnson's motorcade about halfway to Stonewall.

One night it was hailing the size of marbles and we could hardly go over 30 mph. The hail was hitting me in the face and it hurt. I received a call to fall off the escort because the weather was too harsh. I don't know for sure, but I have always thought that order came from the President.

When Johnson was re-elected, Austin threw a big inauguration parade. Once again, we picked up the President at Bergstrom Air Force Base and escorted him into town. When we got to 1st Street and Congress Avenue and moved north toward the Capitol, the avenue was curb-to-curb with people, one of the

[43]

largest crowds we ever had downtown. Pedestrians were crowding in around the motorcade to the point we could hardly move.

I was riding next to the right front bumper of the President's car. We were going at about a walking pace. An agent kept pushing me in the back to go faster. After about six blocks, I began to get tired of that. I stopped my motor, stood up, and told the agent I couldn't just run over the people. If he would like, I added, he could ride the motorcycle and I would push him in his back. I think he got the message. At least I wasn't pushed in the back anymore.

One year during LBJ's presidency, he was celebrating a New Year's Eve in Austin. Sgt. Jack Irwin, Sgt. Mark Cutler, Patrolman Albert Riley, and I were escorting him. We traveled to several locations that evening, and it was getting darned cold on those motorcycles.

We were leaving a house on 24th Street when a Secret Service agent told us to go to a particular address on Enfield Road. By now, it was about 1:30 a.m. on New Year's Day. President Johnson got out of his limousine and walked up to the house, which was dark, and knocked on the door. At the Secret Service's direction, we were standing in a line along the sidewalk going to the house.

After a bit, we saw some lights coming on and a lady came to the door. I heard her exclaim, "My God, it's the President!" Her husband came to the door and invited him in. The President politely declined, saying, "I just wanted to wish you a wonderful New Year. You are a great American."

Then he turned around and left. On his way back to his car, I overheard him say, "Wrong damn address."

About 2:45 a.m., on our way to the Driskill Hotel, one of the Secret Service agents called and said the President was turning in for the night. He said that we were relieved of our duties, and thanked us for our services. I don't know who those people were the President woke up that morning, but I bet they never forgot that night.

My First Excessive Force Complaint

During the 1960s and early 1970s, long before the department had an internal affairs unit, Chief Miles personally investigated almost all complaints against police officers.

One night when I was working the 11 p.m. to 7 a.m. shift, I got a phone call from the chief's office asking me to be in his office at 3 p.m. the next day. Needless to say, I didn't get much sleep after I got off duty.

When I showed up that afternoon, the chief's secretary told me to go in. Inside sat a man I had arrested the night before for DWI. He had his family with him. He also had a patch on his nose between his eyes.

"This gentleman has filed a complaint against you claiming you assaulted him last night," the chief said. "I would like you to tell us your side of the story."

"Chief, sir, I was trying to get his car stopped," I began. "We were going south on IH-35. He took the 1st Street exit, went through a red light at West Frontage Road and 1st Street. He turned left onto 1st Street, hit the esplanade, and ran over a No-Parking sign at which time his car stopped. When I got to his car, he was trying to get out. The collision caused his head to hit the rear view mirror causing the small scratch on the top of his nose. He was intoxicated, had an odor of alcohol, his eyes were fixed and he couldn't get his driver's license out of his billfold."

"I arrested him for DWI, impounded his car, and took a report of the collision where he hit the sign. He was 19 years old and wanted to go home. His injury was very minor with very little blood. After it was cleaned up, it wasn't bleeding. During my investigation, a cab driver stopped to see if he could help. I had him to observe the subject. He also said the driver was intoxicated and observed the minor cut. I didn't record the cab driver's name in the offense report; however, I kept it in my personal notes and I will get it for you." (I learned early on not to put all my witness's names in my reports.)

[45]

Ernie Hinkle

"That is not the way it was explained to me." Miles said. He then asked the complainant to tell his side of the story. The man just said that he wasn't drunk. His father then spoke up and asked me if I had hit his son.

"No Sir," I said, "he was cooperative–he just didn't want to be arrested." At that point, the father took the bandage off his son's nose. The injury was much worse than when I last saw him. The father started asking his son questions, at which time the son broke down. He admitted he had taken the family car out of the garage without his parents' knowledge, went to a party and drank but didn't know he drank too much. He had banged on his head to make it look worse than it was, hoping that would keep him out of trouble with his parents.

After listening to all this, the chief told me I could leave. He followed me out of his office and told me to go home and get some sleep. I said, "Sir, I have all of the arrest information in my offense report." Miles said, "I know–I've read it. I didn't think the complainant was telling the truth and I wanted his parents to know."

Literally a Hot Seat

In the 1960s, our police units did not have a red light on top. All we had to stop a vehicle with was a little hand-held red light. Well, when I got out of my unit to make that arrest that got me in the chief's office, I sat that red light on the seat of my patrol car. By the time I got back to my unit, it had burnt a round hole in the seat and the seat was on fire. I put the fire out, wrote up a city property damage report on the unit, and had to pay $12 to fix the seat. That was my lunch money for the next few days.

Backed Up By Citizens

Austin was growing in the 1960s, but the number of officers hired was not keeping pace. It seemed like we were

[46]

shorthanded all the time. Sometimes on the night shift, we had only eight to ten officers to cover the whole city. Often, if we needed a backup, we would have to ask for one.

At least we didn't have a drug problem like we do today. Alcohol abuse was the big issue then. One night when I was working 11 p.m. to 7 a.m. – the graveyard shift – I received a fight call about 12:30 a.m. at a place called Little Glory's in the 1000 block of East 11th Street.

On arrival, I found the place was full, the crowd mostly male. As I went through the door, I heard someone say, "Hinkle, I got your back." I broke up a fight in the back room and was walking out with a drunk when I heard a commotion behind me. I turned around and saw the man who had said he had my back standing there with a chair in his hands and looking down at someone lying on the floor. Turned out the fellow on the floor had been about to stab me in the back when my unknown buddy cold-cocked him with a chair. I never knew my backup's real name but, on the street, he was known as Red.

The guy Red hit with the chair went to Brackenridge ER and received more than 30 stitches in his head before going to jail. I looked for Red to express my appreciation, but he was gone.

I saw Red about a week later and thanked him for what he had done. He said he liked me and would always take care of me. He said I had helped his girlfriend get her car started when she was out of gas and he felt like he owed me. We became friends and he gave me a lot of information.

For instance, one time I investigated a homicide at East 11th and Curb Streets in East Austin. A transvestite had been stabbed to death about 2 a.m. That part of town was a popular hangout for African-American males dressed up like women. That made for some tricky situations. Once, I had arrested a black female for prostitution. At least I thought "she" was a woman. When I got to the jail, I had a female jailer search her. The jailer immediately came back and said, "Hinkle, you had better search him...she has a rod."

When I arrived at the scene of the homicide a large crowd had gathered; but, as usual, no one had seen anything. EMS declared the subject deceased and I called for a Justice of the Peace to hold an inquest. Subsequently the body was released to the city morgue for Dr. Coleman de Chenar to perform an autopsy. In Texas back then, when there was a suspicious death, a JP was required to come to the scene to release the body. (Today, medical examiners or JPs have that responsibility, depending on the size of the community.)

During my investigation, I happened to see my friend Red standing back in the shadows. I eased over that way. He walked by and told me to meet him on the next corner after everyone left.

I met him a couple of hours later after we had wrapped up our work at the crime scene. Red told me he didn't know the person's name who did the cutting, but that he went by the street name of "Toad." He said the killer had just gotten out of the pen about a week prior to this incident. I wrote all of this information in my offense report.

Lt. Colon Jordan, who headed the homicide unit, got my report the next morning and before noon, he and his men had identified Toad and gotten a warrant for his arrest. Later that day, thanks to Red, the suspect sat in jail.

El Paso Bar

El Paso is in West Texas, but the El Paso Bar used to be in the 1700 block of East 6th Street. Over the years, I made a lot of fight and disturbance calls there. The folks who owned the bar were good people, but they catered to mostly illegal immigrants from Mexico who did a lot of drinking.

On a call in August 1965, I responded to a fight at the El Paso Bar. When I got there, the place was full. Going in, I observed blood over the floor and bar area. I found two subjects lying beside a pool table, very bloody, and still bleeding. EMS took them to the hospital. In trying to find out what happened, everyone I talked to said they were in the bathroom when it happened. I checked out the bathroom and it had one very small commode. Even two or three people would have had a hard time getting in there, much less everyone in the bar. The bartender said he was busy at the time and didn't see anything. I identified several people there and followed up at the hospital.

I finally found out that only the two victims had been fighting. Each came out with a knife and cut the crap out of each other. A female, who I later found out was also involved (she had minor cuts and did not require treatment) had left before I arrived. I was unable to get her identified. I filed on the two subjects at the hospital for fighting.

Over the next two years while working Charlie Sector in East Austin, I enjoyed dealing with the people and stayed busy. I occasionally stopped at Cisco's Restaurant at 1511 East 6th Street. One night about 9 o'clock, I stopped there for coffee. I had just sat down when a man ran in and said there was a fight down the street. Sure enough, it was at the El Paso Bar. I rushed down there and saw a man running across the street with his shirt torn off and another man lying in the street. I checked on him. He had his throat cut from ear-to-ear and was dead.

I followed a trail of blood for about two blocks. Just off 5th Street in the north alley, I found the other suspect. He had run until he was out of blood. He was also dead. Back at the scene, I found a five-inch blade knife. I backtracked looking for another knife but never found one. My guess is that someone picked it up.

Two Missing Three-Year-Olds

One of the saddest calls I ever made was in the 2800 block of Webberville Road. A mother had reported her two three-year-old boys missing. We searched all over the area. I went in a back yard about two houses from where they lived and saw a refrigerator on the back porch. I opened it and saw both little boys were inside, having suffocated. The mother came running down there and we had to restrain her when she realized what had happened.

Ernie Hinkle

I radioed for a Justice of the Peace to meet me at the scene and contacted Human Services to help with the mother. For years, every time I went by that location, in my mind I would see the two little fellows' arms around each other inside that refrigerator.

Time for a "Time Out"

One shift, I responded to a call off the 1900 block of Chestnut in Charlie Sector. When I got there, I was met by a nice woman who told me her 20-year-old son had threatened her with a knife and she wanted him out of her house. She said her boy was a little slow, would sometimes become combative with her and that she needed to get him help. Then we went into the house.

Her son was about six feet tall and weighed at least 230 pounds. Not only that, he had an open five-inch blade knife in his hand. As I began to talk with him, he seemed agitated. But as we kept talking, he seemed to settle down. I asked him for the knife and he gave it to me. I stuck the weapon in my waistband behind my belt, told him I wanted him to go with me, and started to handcuff him.

I got only one cuff on him before all hell broke loose. We wrestled all over the living room. I could tell that he wasn't trying to hurt me; he just wanted to get away. All of a sudden, I realized the open knife I had taken from him was cutting me. I looked down and saw blood. Seeing that, I hollered "Time out!" and he stopped resisting. I took the knife out of my waistband, laid it on the mantle, and the fight was back on.

As I tried to subdue him, his mother kept screaming, "Don't hurt him–he's my baby," and tried to get me off him. Finally, after we had fallen to the floor, I managed to get him rolled up in a throw rug. Only then did his mother calm down. She just didn't want him to get hurt, but that sure wasn't much help for me.

We ended up transferring him to the mental health unit at Brackenridge Hospital for observation. The young man wasn't a bad person, just very confused and mad at the one person who loved him most, his mother.

As for me, I learned another good lesson: Always secure a knife when you have an opportunity. I wasn't cut bad–just two or three scratches that looked worse than they were.

One of the First Civil Rights Protests in Austin

On April 16, 1964, I was called to report to City Hall in the 100 block of West 7th Street to see Sgt. Jack Irwin regarding a disturbance. The sergeant told me that the city council was expecting trouble and he was assembling a few officers to be on hand, if needed.

The NAACP was sponsoring a demonstration intended to pressure the council into passing an ordinance banning racial discrimination. The council was conducting other business when one of the activists, Booker T. Bonner, started talking and would not stop. Mayor Pro-Tem Travis LaRue asked him to take his seat and remain silent, but he refused. At that, Sgt. Irwin, Sgt. Gerald Spohnholtz, and I were told to remove Bonner from the council chamber.

I approached him and asked him to please leave. Instead, he just went limp. We carried him out and laid him down on the sidewalk. Two other demonstrators, the Rev. Wesley Sims and a UT student, also soon found themselves on the sidewalk in front of City Hall. About 15 minutes later, these three tried to crash in the back door of the chambers. Again, we carried them to the sidewalk. After that, they finally decided to leave.

During the rest of the council meeting many people were heard, both pro and con. After things calmed down, two officers remained at City Hall and the rest of us returned to our regular assignments.

Sometime later, I ran into Bonner. He said he was against violence and had only wanted to focus attention on racial inequality.

The first civil rights protest in Austin had been the year before. There was a tavern in the 2600 block of Guadalupe near

Ernie Hinkle

UT called The Pink Lizard. An African-American man had gone in there and was refused service when he tried to buy a drink. The demonstration was small–about a dozen whites supporting The Pink Lizard and about 10 African-Americans wanting the business closed down. Each group marched on the sidewalk outside the bar with their signs.

For some reason, some of the demonstrators exchanged signs, going from pro to con, and pretty soon they were laughing and pointing at each other's suddenly conflicting signs. That outbreak of spontaneous humor broke up the demonstration without us having to make a single arrest. As I remember, within the next few months, the Pink Lizard went out of business.

Cat in the Roadway

I responded to a call in the 6000 block of Cameron Road one shift and found a citizen who was very upset with APD. He told me that a police car speeding past his house had deliberately run down and killed his cat. On top of that, the officer did not stop.

I told the complainant I was sorry and that I would find out who had done that and get back to him.

In checking the calls for that area, I saw that Sgt. Joe Morales had made a disturbance call in the vicinity. I contacted Morales and he told me that he had accidentally run over the cat going to the call. He said he tried to avoid it when it ran out into the road, but it was too late and he just kept going to the call.

I went back and talked to the complainant. I apologized, again, and related the officer's story. It didn't seem to relieve his anger very much and I was running out of options. I told him I was sorry, again, that animals should not be in the roadway, and that this was just an unfortunate accident.

Hoping to calm him down, I asked if I could go to the Humane Society shelter and get him a kitten. "I know it won't take your cat's place, but maybe it will fill a void," I said. Suddenly the man started laughing. "Hinkle," he said, "that was my wife's damn cat. I didn't like it anyway. It was wild and I sure don't want another one."

Everybody Has Got to be Somewhere

One day I received a call to check on a suspicious person on a telephone pole at 45th and Guadalupe Streets. When I arrived, I saw a man on top of a telephone pole. I got out of my unit and asked what he was doing up there.

"Everybody has got to be somewhere," he answered.

"Get down off of that pole," I ordered.

He came down with a little grin on his face.

"Hinkle, I'm Harvey Gann, captain of the vice squad. I have a court order to plant a bug on a telephone line going to a gaming house that we've been watching. I had plenty of probable cause."

"Captain, thank you," I said as I left.

I had heard a lot about the captain, but that was the first time I'd met him. He was a sharp cop, knew what was going on in the city and kept a lid on things.

Shortly after this incident, Capt. Gann called for a uniformed officer to meet him on East 1st Street at Bolm Road. It was around 9 p.m. when I got the call. When I met with him, he said there was an old barn about 300 yards south of 1st Street and that three of his men had been watching a big poker game going on inside it. About a dozen guys were playing, and the house was taking an illegal cut. Gann wanted to sneak up to the barn and catch them in the act. But he wanted someone in uniform to go in first with him.

"Hinkle, they are going to run," he said.

We snuck up to the old barn and when six of his plainclothes officers had the place surrounded, the captain and I broke in making a lot of noise. At that, the gamblers scattered like quail. I flat got run over, but the captain knew what was going to happen and got out of the way. The card players didn't bother going out the door, they went through a wall. The officers outside managed to arrest four of them and I helped take them to jail. The captain was okay with that, telling me the main objective was to keep the gamblers moving.

Gann was a very interesting guy, a great police officer who became an APD legend. During World War II his plane, a B-24 bomber, got shot down over Udine, Italy. Harvey parachuted but was taken as a prisoner of war by the Germans. He escaped and was recaptured seven days later. He escaped and was recaptured two more times before his final attempt succeeded. He later wrote a very thought-provoking book about his experiences during the war, "Escape I Must."

Dude Fisher

One of my first supervisors was Sgt. Dude Fisher, a 40-year police veteran. He was of a small stature, but literally carried a big nightstick. In fact, it looked about as big as he was.

The sergeant always worked security at the wrestling matches at the old City Coliseum on Riverside Drive. One night in 1962, he asked me to help him. We had no problems during the match, but during the intermission, all hell broke out. We had three fights going at the same time.

I got one fight broken up and was looking for the sergeant when I saw him with one of the wrestlers who had been trying to get back to the ring. Several of the spectators were trying to get to the wrestler, throwing chairs and anything else they could. The sergeant had his nightstick out and was whacking anyone who got in his way. We fought our way through the crowd and got inside the ring, thinking that might offer some protection.

We didn't have hand-held radios back then, so we couldn't call for help. Thank God, someone in the crowd phoned headquarters to report the fight. Before long, I saw two officers making their way to us, Sgt. Olan Kelly and Patrolman Bill Landis. Since we were still outnumbered, Sgt. Kelly racked his shotgun. You could hear that very distinctive sound all over the Coliseum, and that calmed everyone down. They stopped the match and we all got out of there.

Shortly after that incident, they quit allowing alcoholic beverages at the matches and the crowds were much easier to police.

Not long after that, Sgt. Fisher said he was going on vacation for a few days. He told me he needed me to go by a house on 15th Street just east of IH-35 to lock up the chickens for the elderly man who lived there. "He doesn't have any chickens," the sergeant explained, "but if we don't go by and tell him they are locked up, he will call the Police Department until an officer comes and tells him that the henhouse is locked."

Also, the sergeant said I was to go by the 4000 block of Avenue A, see a Mrs. Thorp, and tell her the aliens had been removed from her attic. He said that if we didn't do this, Mrs. Thorp would keep calling the watch captain until an officer came to her house.

While the sergeant was gone, as ordered, I went by both locations, locking up the chickens and running off the aliens. I later found out the sergeant had been doing that for two years.

The older gentleman who thought he had chickens died in 1964, but Mrs. Thorp kept us going to her house for years. Finally, Sgt. Greg Lasley, one of the best officers I ever worked with, succeeded in winning her confidence. Telling Mrs. Thorp he was getting rid of those aliens once and for all, he used a "special light" (his flashlight) in her attic and sprayed a little Mace up there for good measure. That seemed to keep the aliens out of her attic but, before long, they started peeking in a window. Time permitting, the officer working Baker Sector in Central Austin would go by and chase off the aliens.

My Former Partner Gets Shot

About 6:30 a.m. on Wednesday, Jan. 29, 1964, I was en route to a traffic assignment when the dispatcher broadcast a message that two officers had been shot during the night shift and that one of them, Don Carpenter, was dead.

Ernie Hinkle

The news hit me hard. Don had been my partner on the walking beat and I had learned a lot from him. He worked hard, was very methodical, always very cautious, and taught me to be the same. Knowing that, I couldn't imagine how he could have been killed.

Earlier that day, about 3 a.m., officers had responded to a call to investigate a burglary at Dean's Drive-In in the 1800 block of South Congress. Officer Bobby Sides was first on the scene and walked to the back of the building. About that time, Don drove up.

Sides said he heard a voice from inside the building saying. "I am coming out. I am coming out with my hands up." Sides called out to Carpenter, "He's coming out." That's when Sides got shot in the chest. Then Don was shot between the eyes without ever seeing the shooter. Officer Sides was able to get off several shots in the direction of the shooter before he slumped to the ground unaware that Don had been shot.

Officer Charlie Wright, one of several officers who responded, spotted a man running away from the back of the tavern. He chased him into an alley, firing several shots at the fleeing figure before he lost him.

Bullet holes in the rear screen door of the building indicated both officers had been shot by someone standing inside a storeroom at the back of the tavern. Inside, Sgt. Olan Kelley and other officers found that several coin machines and the cash register had been ransacked. On the floor was a small pile of change.

The shooter was caught two days later and was subsequently convicted of murder. Officer Sides recovered from his wounds and returned to duty.

At Don's funeral, I felt so sorry for his beautiful wife and little girl. Don was a great officer and a family man. His life had been taken away from him by the useless act of a coward. Those two officers had just been doing their job. But that's the risk all officers take every day and night. After this shooting, I began to take my job even more seriously. I finally truly understood that not all the people we dealt with were going to Sunday school. Don's death also made me appreciate life more, to be a more cautious officer, and more determined than ever to put crooks in jail.

First Try For Promotion

In the 1960s, promotions at APD came few and far between. A lot of the officers were getting old, but they couldn't afford to retire. I remember in 1962 Chief Miles met with all the officers and asked us to go under Social Security. This is the way he approached us in a memo:

> "Fellows [the department had no female officers in the 1960s]: Today I want to ask you to please vote for us to go under Social Security. If you look around, I have older officers who need to retire, but can't afford to. Then I have young officers with young families; and, if something would happen to you, it would be a hardship on your families. I worry about that. So, for those reasons, I am asking you to vote for Social Security. In the long run, I don't know if it is right or wrong; however, for today it is the right thing to do."

We voted to take Social Security and, in a short time, it helped our department by creating vacancies.

Back then, you had to have two years in-grade from the time you completed probation to qualify for promotion. APD gave the test every year, but most of the time there would be only one or two vacancies. An officer got one point added for each year of service. Otherwise, the officer with the highest score got the promotion. There were no other factors considered back then.

In 1964, I was finally eligible to take the sergeant's test. I started studying about three months before the test date, but when the day came, I was too uptight. On top of that, I have never been a good test taker. Not only did I not place on the test, I didn't even pass it. I was devastated and seriously thought about leaving the force. I felt I had let my family down since money was tight. I was only making $340 a month and would have gotten a $40 per month raise if I had scored high enough to make sergeant. Despite the way I felt, I enjoyed police work and my wife and I made the decision that I would keep trying.

I realized I was going to have to better educate myself, so I started going to Central Texas Community College. I would take classes in the morning or at night, whichever patrol shift I was working would permit. I would check out Civil Service books at the public library and read criminal law books. One of my teachers at the college was defense attorney Roy Minton who taught criminal law and was good at it. He would tie it all together to make common sense out of it–something I could understand.

After studying, I felt I had done the best I could to prepare myself to take the next test. That came in 1965 when the department scheduled two tests, one for detective sergeant and one for uniform sergeant. I took both. I missed only one question on the sergeant investigator's test and five questions on the uniform sergeant's test. I came out number one on each test.

Back then, incidentally, the department had only 300 officers and 84 civilian employees.

Chief Miles left it up to me as to which way I wanted to go – plainclothes or uniform. I wanted to stay on the streets and, on March 11, 1966, I got promoted to patrol sergeant. I was one happy camper. Now I knew I could compete on promotional exams and really felt good about my job.

My First Assignment as Sergeant

My first assignment as a sergeant was supervising the Warrant Office, the Leaving the Scene Office, and Lake Patrol. It was mostly working days, which allowed me to be at home with my family at night. I had eight officers in those three units. They were all good men with a lot more longevity than I had.

One problem I did have was that the units were scattered and each one required a different approach. I had two officers in the Warrant Office. They were both in their 60s and spent almost all of their time filing new warrants or on the phone. One of the first things I did was to meet with the sector sergeants. I explained my problem and asked if they could start getting street officers involved in serving the new warrants in their districts. Most all of those warrants were for misdemeanor offenses. Felony warrants went to the Criminal Investigation Division.

The Leaving the Scene Office was in the Traffic Division at headquarters. I had four officers working there. We also followed up on all traffic fatalities, collisions, took cases to court, and inspected taxi drivers for their city licenses. It was a very busy office with something always needing immediate attention. Whenever one of the officers was sick or on vacation, I would fill in for him. That helped me get to know the inner-workings of the office, but there wasn't much more we could do to improve the office with the limited personnel we had.

The Lake Patrol had two officers working on Lake Austin. I worked with them when time would permit. Both officers were retirement age, but couldn't afford to leave. I don't remember what kind of boat we had, but do remember it was in the shop more than it was on the water.

It was during the early and mid-1960s that the Austin Police Association sponsored a Little League baseball league. We had a baseball field on Town Lake at the foot of Canadian Street. It was Thorp Field named after longtime Police Chief Jim "Boss" Thorp. Lt. Glen Garrett took it upon himself to improve the field and to build a clubhouse. Of course, we helped, but Glen made it happen. He was a solid, good officer and one of the best collision investigators I ever worked with. Totally dedicated to the police department, he never married. He also made himself wealthy buying and selling property throughout the city.

Several officers volunteered to coach the teams. Officer Delbert McCullough's team was the Rangers. My team was the Red Caps. A lot of the parents of the players helped coach, as well. Most were from East Austin. We met some great people in a different atmosphere. We had a lot of fun, had six teams, some of which were very good. My friend Ron Habitzreiter with Rooster Andrews Sporting Goods on Guadalupe was instrumental in helping us with T-shirts and some equipment for the teams. Without his support, it would have been hard to field six teams.

The rivalry between the Rangers and the Red Caps was intense, and we would do just about anything to win. I would accuse McCullough of batting some players out of order and he would accuse me of the same thing.

My son, Ricky, was a Red Cap and played second base. He was nine and could hardly throw the ball from second. He is now retired from APD as a commander. What a blessing he is in my life. He has been just a perfect son. My daughter, Vickie, was seven when Ricky was a Little Leaguer. She was his strongest supporter and still is to this day. She is a blessing to our family and to her Dad. In fact, we call her "Saint Vickie."

I spent a lot of time working with the team, but eventually got transferred to the night shift and had to quit coaching.

Ricky went on to play football at Lanier High School, was a good athlete, worked hard, and was a team player. He was voted "Best Team Player" his senior year at Lanier High School. Vickie still is his best supporter. She would tell Ricky he could get up off the ground faster than any player out there. Before Ricky went into law enforcement, he graduated from UT and coached football at Goliad High School in Goliad and at Pflugerville High School in Pflugerville. Vickie also graduated from UT with a degree in social work and has used her education in various ways. She now works with her husband, Greg Baker, in their sign business in Austin.

My Next Assignment

Chief Miles called me to his office one day and said that if I didn't have any objections, he was transferring me to the

Training Division to be class counselor for the 30th Cadet Class. The chief had a way of talking to you that made it hard to disagree with him, but it turned out to be a good job. It was all day work (about 10 hours a day), but I was off most weekends.

We didn't have a training building back then. All classes were at the police station on the first floor in the line-up room. Lt. Pete Weaver instructed most of the classes with the assistance of local FBI agent Ernie Kuhnel and me. It was an excellent class and turned out some fine officers.

Ernie Hinkle

Ernie Hinkle conducting a cadet class.

Graduates of the 30th Session of the Austin Police Academy on July 1, 1966 were (in alphabetical order):

John R. Boyd, Larry G. Crenshaw, Reagan W. Hammett, Don A. Hart, Roger P. Huckabee, James R. Johnson, Waymon E. Lewis, Donald O. Martin, Jr., Dayton Neal, Lloyd C. Polk, Billy G. Schwettman n, Milton Shoquist, Delmar Spoonts, and Sam G. Warren. Others in the picture below are Sgt. Ernie Hinkle (far left), Major B. H. Rosen and Chief R. A. Miles (center), and Lt. R. C. Scott (far right).

Motorcycle Sergeant

After the 30th Cadet Class graduated on July 1, 1966, I was assigned to the Traffic Division as a motorcycle sergeant replacing the man I had worked for on motors, Sgt. Jack Irwin. He left APD to go to Texas Commission on Law Enforcement Standards and Education.

In the late 1960s, the department had two motorcycle shifts. Mark Cutler was the sergeant supervising the second platoon.

We still rode three-wheel Harley Davidsons, which were just about as dangerous as two-wheelers. Sixty to 65 mph was about optimum speed and they were easy to overturn. At first, they were made of black metal, but later the manufacturer started using white fiberglass. Being a little lighter made them somewhat faster, but not much.

A study by the department showed that requests for police service ran highest between 7 p.m. and 3 a.m. Based on that, the schedules for the motorcycle squads were changed. One squad would work a tactical shift during that high-call period. The other squad would work the regular motorcycle shift on days and then rotate with the first squad every 28 days. The motors also were used as a special response team. (APD didn't organize a SWAT team until the 1970s.)

Motorcycle Shift in March 1969 (in no particular order):

Sgt. Ernie Hinkle, Jim Baker, Emcie Eckert, Leonard Snyder, Darrell Gambrell, John Ross, Claude E. Hill, Ernest L. Shugart, Louie W. White, Mike Sinter, John Wolbruck, Roosevelt Sampson, Howard Park, Delmar Spoonts, D. McCullough

[65]

Ernie Hinkle

Sniper on the Tower

The main building at UT, known as the Tower, rises 307 feet — that's 28 stories — above the campus. It is one of the best-known landmarks in the Austin area.

University of Texas Tower, Austin, Texas

For students, the Tower has a variety of meanings: The orange lights displayed after an athletic contest means UT won; the school's Main Library was originally located on the second floor; and, the giant clocks and chimes on top of the Tower are a signal that class is about to begin.

At 11:51 a.m. on Aug. 1, 1966, during class change, the following conversation was recorded by the police telephone switchboard:

"This is Michael Hall at the History Department on the UT Campus. There has been a gunshot on the

Main Plaza outside the Main Building with at least one person wounded."
POLICE OPERATOR: "The Main Plaza?"
MR. HALL: "Yes Sir."

This call initiated one of the bloodiest encounters ever handled by law enforcement officers in Texas. Charles Joseph Whitman, a 24-year-old UT student from Lake Worth, Florida, began his plot the night before when he murdered both his wife and mother. It ended when Officer Ramiro "Ray" Martinez and Officer Houston McCoy shot and killed Whitman on the Tower.

Whitman, a former Marine, planned well. After killing his wife and his mother during the prior night, he purchased additional ammunition and assembled supplies needed for an extended period of time on the fortress-like observation deck of the Tower. These included several weapons, food, water, and extra clothing.

With supplies packed in a trunk, he drove to the Tower, unloaded his equipment, secured a hand truck, and rolled his trunk down the hallways to the Tower elevators. Many people saw him doing that, but most of them gave him no more than a casual glance since it was not unusual for deliverymen to follow the same route.

On arrival at the 27th floor, which was as high as the elevator would go, Whitman removed his trunk from the elevator and carried it up the narrow stairway to the observation deck. Sometime during this period, he fatally wounded the receptionist on duty and shot four visitors approaching the observation deck from the stairs. He then barricaded the stairway entrance with the receptionist's heavy desk, tied one rifle to the south parapet, and at approximately 11:50 a.m., began firing at the human targets on the broad plaza below.

Before Whitman was taken out by Martinez and McCoy, he had killed 16 people and wounded 31 more.

Approximately five minutes after the original call was received, one of the first officers at the scene, Billy Speed, was immediately shot and died at the scene. Other officers confirmed that one or more persons were firing at random from the top of the Tower.

All available units were dispatched to the UT area with instructions to first seal the area off as nearly as possible to both vehicular and pedestrian traffic. Simultaneously, all ambulance companies were dispatched to pick up the wounded. (Back then, Austin had only private ambulances operated by local funeral homes, not city-staffed medical units.)

Criminal Investigation Division detectives were sent to the scene with old .35-caliber rifles (which was the only rifle the department was equipped with at that time) to pin the sniper down. The regular police-issue weapons, revolvers, and shotguns were useless because of the range. With a scoped, high-powered rifle, Whitman had the officers out-gunned.

The department's communications section was double-staffed as quickly as possible and, during the time Whitman was firing, no calls for police services were answered unless violence was involved.

Calls were made to other law enforcement agencies such as the Travis County Sheriff's Department and the Texas Department of Public Safety, both of which immediately assigned all available personnel to assist.

A local pilot volunteered his plane for observation purposes. APD Lt. Marion Lee and civilian pilot Jim Boutwell radioed that there was only one person on top of the Tower. On their first pass, Whitman put two rifle bullets through the fuselage of their plane before they were able to get out of range.

Communication with the officers at the scene was not good. Officers who had managed to get into the base of the Tower had to use telephones. Portable radios for all officers would not become standard issue until the 1970s. All APD had back then were some World War II surplus "walkie-talkies." To make matters worse, all telephone trunk lines to the department were jammed from incoming calls from the public and out-of-city news media.

All available off-duty officers were recalled. Many of them had already voluntarily returned when the news was flashed from local radio and television stations. Checks were made with military establishments for armored vehicles, but none were available.

About 1 p.m., a squad of men was dispatched from the UT security office with the primary objective of removing the wounded from the stair landing on the 27th floor. The group worked their way through a series of utility tunnels to the base of the Tower. They arrived at the 27th floor shortly after another group of officers and civilians who had gathered independently and made their way up into the building.

Finally, at 1:24 p.m., 92 minutes from the time the original call came in, the following radio transmission was received:

"Unit 34 to Headquarters. We have got that man!"

Without the heroic work of the public, members of local business firms, and other law enforcement groups in the area, the situation could have lasted much longer with even more casualties.

Like most real heroes, they did not wait around to give their names and describe what their actions were. Many were students and some were ambulance drivers. For 90 minutes they all had one thing in common–they were caught in a hail of gunfire and all around them lay bleeding victims who needed help. Some tried to help only to be struck down by a gunman who clearly was picking his victims, not firing randomly.

Ernie Hinkle

Weapons and Other Gear Carried by Whitman

The Inventory Included:

7 Guns
> Rifle - 6mm Bolt Action - Remington - with Telescope
> Sight
> Rifle - 35 cal. Pump - Remington
> Rifle - 30 cal. M-1 Government Issue
> Shot Gun - 12 Gauge Automatic - Sears Roebuck -
> Barrel and Stock Sawed off
> Revolver - 357 Mag. - S & W
> Automatic Pistol - 9mm Luger
> Automatic Pistol - 6.35mm Galesi - Brescia

Large Quantity of Ammunition
Radio
3 ½ Gallons of Water
3 ½ Gallons of Gasoline
4 Knives
1 Hammer
1 Hatchet

Alarm Clock
Transistor Radio
12 cans of Food
Lengths of Wire and Rope
Ear Plugs

The Small Part I Played in the Tower Incident

Around noon, I was on my three-wheeler in about the 6000 block of North Lamar, just past the DPS Headquarters, when I received a call from Capt. Buddy Fann that there was a sniper on the Tower. I quickly turned around and headed south toward the campus. When I reached the 2900 block of Guadalupe, I began hearing rifle fire, the shots coming about 10 to 20 seconds apart.

At the intersection of 24th Street and Guadalupe, people were sitting in their cars. I asked them to please leave their vehicles parked at the intersection and get inside a building somewhere. After I told them why, that a sniper was on the Tower, they were glad to go for cover. About that time, I saw a pedestrian in the 2200 block of Guadalupe in front of the Co-op get shot.

By this time, the other motorcycle officers in my squad had pretty much sealed the traffic flow off. Motorcycle units were at 19th Street (now MLK), 21st, and Guadalupe, 22nd and 23rd off Guadalupe. The officers knew they had to seal the area off -- they didn't need to be told what to do. I rode the entire area making sure all traffic was stopped.

I then went back to 24th Street at the north entrance to the campus. My first thought was to go after the shooter on the Tower. I got off my motorcycle and walked to the north side of the main mall. I could see several injured people lying on the apron of the West Mall and started to go help them, but I couldn't get to them because of the rapid shots still coming down from the Tower.

I ran back to my motor and got out of there. I saw an armored car at San Jacinto and 24th and asked the driver to go with me to the Tower. He said he would be glad to help. To this day, I don't know the driver's name, but the department did later give the armored car service a plaque for their service.

We proceeded to Little Campus Drive off 24th. I left my motor there and got in the armored vehicle. We went to the West Mall and I picked up a young man whose arm was barely hanging on. He asked me about his arm. I tied his arm against his body with his belt and pulled him into the vehicle. Ambulances were at 24th and Whitis, so I took him to that location and transferred him to an ambulance. I went back and picked up two or three more injured people. Along the way, Officer Charles Baylor joined me and helped load other injured persons. I saw students carrying the wounded to shelters at the risk of their own lives.

Even after the broadcast that the sniper had been shot, gunfire continued. When I didn't see any more injured people, I went back to my motor and began to ride Guadalupe from 25th Street going south. That's when I understood why I was still hearing gunshots. In addition to DPS officers and state game wardens, a lot of civilians had shown up with deer rifles and were still shooting toward the Tower. These well-intentioned volunteers had not yet heard that the sniper was dead.

Somewhere around 22nd and Guadalupe, I saw a civilian still shooting. I rode up to him and told him the sniper had been shot. "No," he said, "The guy was waving a white flag on the observation deck." The citizen said he didn't want the bastard to give up–he needed to be shot. I finally got him to quit shooting and later found out that one of the officers on the tower had put a white handkerchief on the end of a rifle and waved it hoping to alert people to stop shooting.

By the time I made it around the perimeter, all shooting had finally stopped. I headed for the north entrance to the Tower where I met Detective Lt. George Phifer and several officers bringing Whitman's body down. They loaded him into an ambulance and I escorted the body to the coroner's office.

That day changed many peoples' lives. There were many heroes – law enforcement officers, students and other civilians.

I could not be more proud of our department. We were not equipped to handle an incident of that magnitude, but without the kind of officers we had, the day could have been much worse. Thanks to APD and other officers, after the first 25 to 30 minutes, Whitman had been pinned down and was not able to shoot as accurately if at all.

Several officers and citizens received medals from the department for what they did on that terrible day. I was presented a Meritorious Conduct Bar, but the real heroes were those officers and civilians who made their way to the Tower. All these years later, I still do not like to be around the Tower.

Cadet Drives Motorcycle into Town Lake

One of the motorcycle sergeant's duties was teaching all police cadets how to ride a three-wheeler. On Saturday, March 11, 1967, I was instructing the cadet class. They got four hours of classroom instruction before we went out in the field to drive the units. With 15 cadets in the class, I would take five to the field at a time. Helping me with the training was Lt. Robert Scott and Officer Harold Rigby.

We would practice riding at the foot of Canadian Street on the north side of Town Lake, a wide-open area about a hundred yards from the water. We told the cadets to take their time just getting used to the operation of the unit, particularly familiarizing themselves with the fact that the off switch was in front of them on the gas tank.

Cadet Howard Hall was about the fourth cadet to operate the unit. Howard started off, just froze, and headed straight for the water. The closer he got to the lake, the faster he went. I jumped on my motor and tried to catch him, but Howard and the three-wheeler shot off into the lake. He went in the water and the motor came down on top of him.

I went in the water and pulled Howard out to the bank and Lt. Scott got him the rest of the way out. Another officer rushed him to Brackenridge ER where Dr. Bud Dryden put several stitches in Hall's forehead. He was pretty beat up, but had no broken bones. By the time I got to Brackenridge, Chief Miles was already there. I explained to him what had happened and he agreed that no negligence had been involved. Hall had simply frozen up. The chief also said we had done a good job getting him to the ER as quickly as we did. I wrote a report, and that was the end of it.

Cadet Hall went on to graduate and became one of the finest criminal investigators APD ever had, and we had some great ones.

Leaving the Scene of a Collision

Like the old saying goes, crime does not pay. Neither does trying to cover up an offense.

In February 1967, a collision occurred downtown in the 1200 block of Colorado. Not long after that, someone reported that a damaged 1948 Ford truck was parked in the 2400 block of Leon Street. Officer Jerry Spain and I located the owner of the truck and he admitted that he had been involved in a wreck on Colorado. Then he told us the story behind it.

After the wreck, some boys in a white Plymouth stopped and asked, "Would you like to beat this?" Being very drunk, he liked that idea. So, the helpful boys started pushing his Ford west on 12th Street. He managed to get it started and drove to the 2400 block of Leon.

The next day, he and some friends rented a truck and towed the nearly 20-year-old Ford to San Antonio. There he bought a left front fender to replace the one knocked off in the collision. After they pulled the 1948 truck back to Austin, they put the fender on. But since one of the doors had also been damaged, the replacement part didn't fit very well.

So, he and his friends drove to New Braunfels, paid $65 for another 1948 Ford truck that would not run and pulled it back to Austin. He took the license plates off the truck involved in the collision and put them on the inoperable Ford.

He told us he figured his odds of not getting caught were about 90 percent after all that. He also said the night of the collision, some of his friends went back to the scene and picked up the beer cans that he had kicked out of the truck. He then buried them. Despite all his effort to cover up his traffic violations, he ended up with citations for making an unsafe right turn (which led to the collision) and leaving the scene of a collision. The money and time he spent trying to avoid getting caught amounted to more than the fines he had to pay.

Arresting a Senator

Merely doing my job, I got involved in some cases I would just as soon have missed. I am sure other officers have felt the same. One arrest I made became political fast. This is how I laid it out in my offense report:

> On April 20, 1969 at approximately 1:15 a.m., I was stopped northbound at the curb of 19th and Red River. I observed a 1969 Chrysler with a black top and light green bottom traveling southbound on Red River hit the west curb, bounce off of it, and then hit the curb again approximately one-half block down the street. By the time I could get turned around, the vehicle was out of sight. I proceeded south on Red River and again observed the same vehicle in the 900 block of Red River. There was a white car behind the Chrysler. I passed the white car and observed the Chrysler hit a parked and unattended Cadillac sitting at the west curb southbound in the 800 block of Red River. I went over to the driver of the Chrysler— the only person in the car—and asked if he was hurt. He stated he was not, that he had "bumped it a little." I asked the driver to get out of the car and as he got out, he had to hold onto the door. We walked around to the front of the car, with the driver bracing himself against his car, to look at the damage. He stated it was okay, he could drive

it. The right front fender and bumper were up against the tire making it impossible to drive it. I advised him he would need a wrecker. He again looked at the car and stated he would drive it. I asked the driver for his driver's license. He was identified as Charles N. Wilson, white male, 36. I then placed Mr. Wilson under arrest and advised him of his rights, Article 15:17, Code of Criminal Procedure. He had a strong odor of an alcoholic beverage, eyes glassy, very unsteady on his feet; his reactions were slow—didn't seem to know where he was. He had trouble getting his driver's license out of his pocketbook. He stated he had about two beers. When asked if he knew what happened, he stated he "bumped it a little." His mental status was polite and cooperative. When asked about the blood test, he stated, "It is up to you." I don't feel he was in a condition to make a decision at the time—blood test declined. Wilson stated he had a shot for a cold this morning. Photo taken at the scene. The driver of the white car mentioned earlier stopped at the scene, gave his name as Donald Seilheimer, white male, stated he had been following the Chrysler for some distance, that he was going all over the road, that he felt like the driver was drunk, that he would testify to same or do whatever he needed to do. He did not observe the driver, only a drunk vehicle. Police Buddy (civilian rider), W. J. Speed, riding with this officer, observed Wilson to be drunk, and also the drunk vehicle. Officer Mills made investigation of the collision. Lt. Garrett observed Wilson at the scene. The vehicle Mr. Wilson was driving was a 1969 Chrysler with a black top and light green bottom, Texas SO-29, the same vehicle I observed hit the curb just before the collision. I was attempting to get the vehicle stopped before it was involved in the collision, but didn't make it.

Collision occurred approximately 1:15 to 1:30 a.m..''

About an hour later, I got a call from the watch commander, Capt. Wilfred Swinney. The captain told me several state officials were in the front lobby wanting to know if they could have the senator released to them. Swinney said it was my call and he would support whatever decision I made.

At about 2:45 a.m. after Sen. Wilson had processed through jail, I took him down to the front lobby. On the way, he was polite and he seemed to have sobered up some. He said he had two beers at the Villa Capri about two hours previous. I told him I was going to release him, but to be back at the police station at 9 a.m. Sunday.

When we reached the front lobby, eight to ten men were there. They started asking if the senator had been beaten and making comments about how Wilson looked. The senator said nothing in my defense and it made me angry, since I was trying to give him a break.

"I am sorry he got arrested," I said in a loud voice. "I'm the arresting officer. I don't abuse anyone. He was drunk, driving a car and had a wreck. I can put him back in jail and he can go before the judge in the morning."

It got quiet and Sen. Charles Herring, whose district included Austin and Travis County, spoke up and asked if Wilson could be released to him, and I agreed to do that. When he returned to the station the next morning, Wilson was charged with first-offense driving while intoxicated. Municipal Court Judge Ronnie Earle warned him of his rights and then released him on personal recognizance.

The next day, the Austin American-Statesman ran an article headlined, "D.W.I. Filed on Senator Charles Wilson from Dist. Three Lufkin Area." Boy, did that open a can of worms. I began to get calls from all over Texas wanting to know more about the arrest, and how I had been treated by the senator. I told them the case was in the hands of the County Attorney, Ned Granger.

Ernie Hinkle

Chief Miles called me and said he was behind me 100 percent, that he had read my report, had received several calls about the arrest, and that I was doing my job. I also got a call from the editor of the newspaper, Sam Wood. He also said that he was behind me and that if I received much pressure over the arrest, to let him know.

About two weeks later, Wilson's attorney called me and wanted to take me out for dinner. I told him I would meet him at my home or at the police department. He came by my house and said that the senator had praised me for my courtesy and that I did what he would have done. The attorney went on to tell me that some people had called the newspapers in the senator's home district and that some of the larger dailies had been publishing distorted versions of the incident. In other words, Wilson's political enemies were trying to use this case against him. He went on to say that Wilson had a lot to offer the people of Texas and that he was a good person doing a good job.

Telling me that Wilson was well-backed by a big East Texas timber company and that a DWI conviction would not go well in that part of the state, he said they didn't want to go to trial and asked what I thought about the case. I told him it didn't matter to me what happened. It was in the hands of the county attorney's office and I was ready to testify that the senator had been drunk. I explained I had a "drunk" car that became involved in a collision while I was trying to get it stopped and that I then had to help Wilson out of the vehicle.

The attorney asked where my case was the weakest. I thought about it–my case was strong and I was ready to go to trial. I wasn't going to change a thing. He kept repeating how the arrest was being used politically against Wilson. I then told him that in my offense report, I wrote that I had asked the senator if he was sick, a by-the-book question. He had told me that he wasn't ill but that he had an injection that morning for allergies and was also taking sinus pills. The attorney thanked me and said he thought they now had a way out.

Shortly after this meeting, County Attorney Granger called me. "Ernie," he said, "I got some issues with our case." He said that Wilson had sent him a letter from his doctor saying the shot he got for hay fever could last for 24 hours, and that he had received two affidavits from men who were with the senator shortly before he left the party. Both men said that he wasn't drunk.

On top of that, Granger said that Tarrant County Sheriff Lon Evans had been with the senator and said that he wasn't drinking that night. Granger told me that just after the arrest, Sen. Herring had told him that Wilson would plead guilty to a lesser charge. Granger then asked if I would change the charge from DWI to DUID (Driving Under the Influence of Drugs). I told him those "drugs" sure smelled like alcohol to me. I said that I would support any decision he made, but that I would not change the charge.

Granger ended up changing the case to DUID and Wilson didn't have to worry so much about what all the Baptists in East Texas would think about him drinking and driving while representing them in Austin.

The senator pled guilty to DUID before County Court-at-Law Judge Jerry Dellana and was fined $200. At a press conference afterward, Wilson produced the letter from his doctor saying he had received heavy doses of drugs for hay fever. "There was no deal made," he said. "I pled guilty for DUID because I felt I was guilty."

I really got an insight into politics in this case. During my investigation, Wilson had been cooperative, polite, and at no time did he question anything that was being done. He did not ask for any special favors or even hint he wanted one, but I can't say that about some of the people around him or even some others in law enforcement.

Wilson went on to serve 12 years in the Legislature and 24 years in Washington as a Congressman. He went on to earn the nickname of "Good Time Charlie," but also almost single-handedly put together a mini-war that resulted in the defeat of Russia in Afghanistan. They made a movie about that called "Charlie Wilson's War." He was a flamboyant person who had an eccentric lifestyle.

In October 1996, at an Angelina County Chamber of Commerce luncheon in Lufkin, Wilson announced that he was resigning from Congress. He thanked the crowd of more than 500 people for their support over the past 36 years and apologized for his occasional rowdy behavior while in office. The crowd gave him a standing ovation, chanting, "We've had a Good Time Charlie." Wilson died February 10, 2010.

I never talked to him after the night of the arrest. I saw him a few times after that, but kept a low profile. I always respected him. We all make mistakes.

Working Anti-War Protests

In addition to traffic assignments, funeral escorts, various other types of escorts and ball games, the motorcycle unit worked the anti-war protests that began as the Vietnam War grew worse.

The Austin chapter of the SDS (Students for Democratic Society) was very active. At times, the protestors would just take over a street or intersection without a permit. Sometimes, however, they did have a permit and our job was to escort them and hopefully prevent trouble. There was also the problem of trying to protect them from members of the public who were not sympathetic to their cause. At times, there could be between 3,000 to 4,000 protestors.

The majority of protestors were good students who were just championing a cause. The problem for law enforcement came when the crowd began following a leader. Its members would forget their individual identity and turn into a mob. In most cases, if we could arrest the leader, the crowd would begin to break up.

We sometimes had to use teargas and officers took a lot of abuse. We got spat on numerous times and were known more often as "pigs" rather than cops. We just had a job to do and did not let their harassment get personal. I was very proud of our officers who I think always exercised restraint in dealing with these mostly young people.

Unlawful Assembly

About 9 a.m. on May 5, 1970, University of Texas Police Chief Cannon advised APD that a large group was gathering on the main mall at the UT Tower to hold an anti-war protest rally at noon. He said he had information that the group would be leaving the campus and marching to the Capitol and then south on Congress Avenue to downtown.

At that time, the crowd was estimated to be around 1,000 people made up of two groups—the Student Mobilization Committee and the Students for a Democratic Society.

As the rally began, Major Bruce Biggerstaff briefed all APD officers in the assembly room as to intelligence received up until that time. It had been established that the group did not have a permit to get in the streets. But as long as they protested peaceably and stayed on the sidewalks, the police would assist them.

I assembled our platoon of approximately 16 motorcycle officers. Each officer was armed with teargas grenades and gas masks. We would flank the group when they left the campus. Other police officers were on standby to be available if needed.

By about 1:30 p.m. the crowd was growing. Some of the speakers were hostile and some were peaceful. We were advised by our intelligence source that the crowd was still building. One of the speakers was being very hostile, urging the crowd to take over Congress Avenue.

Then the crowd began to move. They went north on the UT campus to 24th Street, then west on 24th to Guadalupe. At the intersection, the crowd was told to stay out of the roadway and on the sidewalks. They headed south on Guadalupe and took over the street in the 2200 block. I formed a line of motorcycle officers across the intersection of Guadalupe and 19th Street (now MLK). But the large crowd overran our line and I called the officers to move back to the intersection of Congress and 15th Street. As the crowd was going east on 19th, some vehicular traffic got caught up in the crowd and the street was completely full of protestors for several blocks.

I saw a brown pickup surrounded by protestors who began banging on his truck and walking on the hood. One of the protestors broke his radio antenna. At that, the driver got out of his truck and started running after the guy who broke the antenna. He caught him at 19th Street and University Boulevard and was kicking his butt. I ran over to break the fight up. The driver, a male in his early 30s, was some pissed off. By then a large crowd had encircled us. We were getting hit with rocks, stomped on, cursed at, and hit in the back.

"Officer, if you will hold these SOBs off of me, I will whip all of them one at a time," the driver said. I told him to calm down. We were in a bad spot and needed to get out of there. Somehow we fought our way back to his truck. Once in his truck, he revved the motor, started smoking his tires, and took off at a high rate of speed. I thank God he didn't run over anyone as the street was still full of protestors. I never got the driver's name. I was too busy trying to get him out of there. Whoever he was, I would be proud for him to back me up anytime.

From 19th the crowd turned south on Congress. I caught up with our motorcycles and followed through with my plan to set up a line of officers across the intersection of Congress Avenue and 15th. At this location, we were joined by Capt. Don Doyle's shift (now Chief Don Doyle, retired). Despite the additional manpower, the police line was again overrun. The only slight positive was that some of the crowd broke up by running around our flanks.

By then, the protestors were estimated to be between 1,500 to 1,800 people strong. All officers were told to gather at 11th Street and Congress Avenue. The students had now changed from an expressive crowd to a mob. They went around the Capitol and continued going south toward Congress on the main walkway. Along the way, two vehicles parked on the Capitol grounds had been firebombed.

Capt. Robert Wilke's platoon of approximately 35 officers along with Sgt. Abner Schulle had re-assembled at 11th and Congress. I deployed the motor officers in a skirmish line across the intersection facing the demonstrators and Capt.

Wilke's officers filled in behind us. We finally got the demonstrators stopped at the intersection. But they were throwing bottles, rocks, and anything else they could find. When the first protestor stepped off the curb, we started using the teargas.

Their eyes burning, the protestors broke up and started running back the way they had come. We made six arrests for being in the roadway, a misdemeanor. Now running back north, some of the protestors entered the Capitol, apparently hoping to hole up in there. But one gas grenade moved them out through the north door on the backside of the building. They kept running north on Congress with the police right behind them.

At 19th and Congress, the demonstrators again stopped. Gas was again used and they finally disbursed in all directions.

We walked back to 11th and Congress to get our motorcycles then rode back to 19th Street and Congress. I then met with Capt. George Phifer (now retired as Acting Chief). Phifer advised me he had talked with one of the group leaders, Jeff Freidman, who had been trying to keep the march peaceful. Freidman told him the march was over and the students were returning to campus.

I got to know Freidman personally and he would quite often ride along with me when I was in a district car. He later went on to become Austin's youngest-ever mayor.

The situation that day had come close to really getting out of hand. If the protestors had made it to the downtown area, they would have been very destructive. The students had lost their identity as individuals and taken on the mood of the crowd. But our officers did a good job. They took a lot of abuse and definitely earned their pay that day.

Citizen Takes Up Traffic Law Enforcement

I received a call one day in May 1969 to go to the 100 block of West 34th St. where a citizen was stopping vehicles. On my arrival, I saw a man with a rifle walking up and down the north sidewalk. He had just stopped a vehicle as I drove up.

Since he wasn't pointing the weapon at me, I kept my pistol in my holster and walked up to him. When I approached him, he gave me the driver's license of the driver of the car he had stopped and wanted me to issue the man a ticket for speeding. The driver was Jerry Day who just happened to be an off-duty Austin police officer. Jerry wanted to know what was wrong with the man, but I told him that I would take care of it and he left at my request.

In talking with the man, I quickly realized he had an obsession about speeding vehicles and just wanted to help the police with a little citizen law enforcement. He had a notebook with maybe a dozen license plate numbers written in it and wanted me to check registration on the plates and file on the drivers for speeding. When I asked him what proof he had the cars had been speeding, he asked me to sit on his front porch with him and he would show me.

To calculate the speed of a vehicle, you need time and distance, and this guy clearly knew that. He had set up a pole at the end of the block and another one about mid-block. When a vehicle passed the first pole, he would start his stopwatch and stop it when it reached the other pole. Then he would calculate the speed of the car. I actually made a test run in my police car as he checked a passing vehicle and he was correct in coming up with its speed his way.

I learned he was a math instructor at UT, lived alone, and was very smart, but had some hang-ups about society. I told him I would make a deal with him. I wanted him to put his rifle up and quit stopping the vehicles. I pointed out the danger in what he was doing and asked him not to take the law into his own hands. He stowed his rifle and said he would not stop vehicles anymore, but asked if he could sit on his front porch and time the vehicles going by for speeding. He then wanted to know if he could call me and give me the license numbers. I told him I would not issue anyone a ticket if I had not witnessed the violation. But I also told him I would periodically come by to visit him and that I would have a motorcycle officer work radar at that location.

Back at the station, I found out that he had called the Police Department more than 15 times in the past week complaining about speeding vehicles. About two weeks later, I went by to visit him. He gave me five license plate numbers and I told him I would come by about once a month to pick up information he had. For several months, I would stop by to visit him and he would give me a few tag numbers. I would put them in my files. He stopped calling the department and, after a few months, he gave up timing the vehicles altogether. I think he thought he had the speeding under control. The police need all the help they can get from the public, but he took it just a little too far.

Justifying Motorcycles

In 1969, Chief Miles, who I believe was one of the best chiefs I ever worked for, sent me a memo asking me to justify the price of the new three-wheel motors. His budget was tight and he was thinking of possibly doing away with motors altogether.

It bothered me that we had to justify the motors since I knew we were doing just a great deal of work on them. Most of the motor officers were very dedicated and worked hard in all types of weather. Earlier that year we had received six new Harley Davidson units which were equipped with police packages from Austin Motorcycle Company, owned by P. R. James. The units cost $2,330 each--$13,992 for all six. We traded six old units in for $200 each.

We had 20 three-wheelers and would trade in six or seven units every two years for new ones. The old units would be pretty worn out with around 45,000 to 55,000 miles on each.

I did research on the work of our motorcycle unit and this is how I justified them in a memo back to the chief:

1. It would be hard, and in some cases almost impossible, to escort in a car. Other than funeral escorts, our department was often called

on to escort large trucks with oversized loads, houses being moved, and VIPs. On UT football game days or nights, we would make eight to ten escorts, including team buses, bands, mascots, and a number of other buses. In 1969, motors handled 1,388 funeral escorts. I felt that was a service our department provided for the families at no cost to them.

2. Motors work in rainy and hazardous weather and are usually the first units on the scene of collisions where the wrecked cars can be moved and an officer can direct traffic to open up the streets.

3. Each motorcycle is taken home by the officer assigned to it. The officer is in service at the time he leaves home to go to work until he gets home from work. This saves overtime because the officer is available for calls and in a position to work traffic more than just eight hours.

4. The motorcycle shifts work mostly 8 a.m. to 5:30 p.m.; however, the hours are flexible and are changed when needed to meet the workload.

5. Motors are also used as a tactical force. The motor officers have received intensive training in controlling crowds and riots and unusual occurrences. While the motorcycle unit is made up of 10.4 percent of the total of the department's commissioned officers, in 1968 the unit wrote 18.8 percent of all reports and made 21.1 percent of all arrests. They also issued 39.9 percent of all citations issued by the department.

6. I noted a recent instance when the motor unit had been mobilized at night, responding within twenty minutes fully equipped to handle a situation involving a barricaded person.

I said that in my opinion, the motorcycle unit was one of the most important units the department had. However, I did recommend that the officers could use some warm clothes in the winter, especially leather jackets and leather gloves.

I never heard back from the chief and the department never furnished me or my officers a leather jacket, but the motorcycle unit is still going strong to this day.

UT Football Riots

During the 1970s, it seemed every time that UT won a football game at Royal Memorial Stadium, a large crowd gathered along Guadalupe Street on the west side of the campus to celebrate. In those days, UT had great teams. Winning was expected, and most of the time the Longhorns did. The majority of those in the post-game crowds were students just out to have a good time, but quite often outsiders would come in trying to cause trouble. Some agitators in the crowd could change the crowd from expressive to aggressive pretty quickly.

The motorcycle shifts would move over to the Guadalupe Street area after a game was over and traffic had cleared out of the stadium area.

On January 1, 1970 at about 7 p.m., there were between 400 to 500 people gathered in the 2200 to 2300 blocks of Guadalupe. The Longhorns had just beaten Notre Dame in the Cotton Bowl at Dallas. Some in the crowd started throwing bottles at passing cars and, especially, at police officers. The crowd began to come out into the street stopping traffic, breaking radio antennas off vehicles, beating on car hoods, and, in general, raising hell.

I sent two plain-clothed officers into the crowd, David Neeley and Warren Templeton. They began to pick out the troublemakers and we would go in the crowd and arrest them. We put the word out that we had a lot of undercover officers in the crowd and, before long; we got folks under control and out of the street. We made 12 arrests that night, all misdemeanors.

Some after-game celebrations got out of control and we had to use teargas to break the crowds up. I hated the gas, since I could never get my mask on fast enough. One time I accidentally dropped a gas grenade. Next thing I knew I was on my knees next to Unit 202 crying and throwing up. Of course, my misfortune was the laugh of the day at headquarters.

As time went on, we got smarter and would just shut Guadalupe down between 21st to 24th Streets and walk the perimeter on the west side. After two to three hours, we would open the street back up. That seemed to work well. Fewer arrests were made, the students got to celebrate, and very little, if any, property damage occurred.

Arresting the UT Chancellor

On Sunday, December 19, 1971 at about 12:45 a.m., Officer Don Martin called and asked me to meet him at the city jail. In those days, it was the procedure that anyone arrested for DWI had to be interviewed by a supervisor.

A very dedicated and professional officer, Don told me he had been trying to stop a "drunk" vehicle headed north in the 2500 block of Guadalupe. The vehicle, a 1972 black Cadillac, had been moving really slow and holding up traffic. It also had been weaving lane-to-lane. When Don tried to stop the driver for running a red light at 26th Street, the car almost ran into the back of a stopped vehicle. When the light turned green, the Cadillac accelerated, spinning its rear wheels. That made the car slide hard to the right. Don said the Cadillac had almost run into his police unit twice as he tried to get the vehicle to pull over.

Even though the officer had his unit's red light and siren on, the Cadillac kept going. Finally, he told me, the driver pulled into the El Patio Restaurant parking lot in the 2900 block of Guadalupe and stopped.

When I met Don at the jail, I learned that he had arrested Frank Erwin, chancellor of the UT system. The chancellor had a strong odor of an alcoholic beverage and was unsteady on his

[88]

feet. I warned him of his rights, took a picture of him, and asked him two times if he would take a breath test. Both times, he declined.

Erwin said he didn't want to take a test of any kind. He knew he was drinking, but said he wasn't drunk and wanted to know why we were doing this to him. I asked what he was drinking. He said, "Well, hell, scotch and soda at a Christmas party." Then I asked when he had his last drink. He answered, "Just before I saw you." He added, "This is foolishness, why are you doing this to me."

I took him to the booking desk and helped him sit down on a bench. While I was waiting my turn to book him, he fell off the bench. I assisted him in getting up and stayed with him until he was booked. Meanwhile, another officer drove his car to the police pound.

Erwin's attorney, Larry Temple, got him out of jail just after he was booked. Municipal Judge Jon Coffee charged him with first offense DWI and released him on personal bond.

I was proud of Don for making the arrest and the way he handled the situation. The chancellor had been in no condition to be driving -- for his own safety and the safety of the driving public. To his credit, unlike many drunks, at no time did he act abusively or be uncooperative. He was just drunk.

Several months later, I was subpoenaed to meet with Attorney Roy Minton to give a deposition in the case. I knew Roy Minton and Charles Burton, his partner, well. I had taken several criminal law courses under Minton at Central Texas College. I also had been the arresting officer in quite a few cases his law firm had tried.

Thanks in part to what I had learned from him, and by experience, I had a history of making good arrests. I showed respect for the people I had arrested, and I always answered questions looking directly at the jury. A lot of trial attorneys got their tricks from a red book called "Defense for D.W.I." I bought that book and studied it to prepare myself before a trial.

At the deposition, Roy didn't ask many questions, but in some ways, he took me to the cleaners. He's a sharp attorney. In a joking way, he asked if I had ever made a DWI arrest that I might have regretted. I answered, "I prefer not to make an arrest, if possible; however, if the subject is drunk and driving a vehicle, it is our job to get them off the streets." I wish I had just stopped there, but I began to tell him about the letter I had received years ago from a lady I had arrested for DWI. She thanked me for the way I treated her and reported that her test result came back with a blood-alcohol level of 0.06 percent. At that time, the legal limit for intoxication was 0.10 percent blood-alcohol. The case against that woman had been dropped, but I told Roy that in my opinion the lady had been driving very erratically and was intoxicated.

At that point, Minton asked me to go over that 1962 arrest for him, and I did. (I told the story earlier in this book.) Minton then asked if there were other cases similar to this. I had a record of making a lot of DWI arrests and a good conviction rate. My attitude was, if the driver was drunk and driving, he or she went to jail.

I shared the only other case I could think of with him, also mentioned earlier in this book, in which I arrested a man who seemed obviously drunk only to learn later that he was a diabetic having major blood sugar issues. Since he hadn't gone before the judge yet, charges were never filed and I marked the report as "unfounded."

With that, Minton ended the deposition. A few months later, I learned from the court clerk that Minton had requested a change of venue and that my case against Erwin would be tried in Killeen. A month or two after that we went to court there. When I saw the jury, I knew I was in trouble. All of them were men who looked like they were late to happy hour.

When I testified, Minton asked why I thought Erwin had been drunk. I went over the normal testimony – "drunk" car, odor of alcohol, staggering, didn't remember where he was going, and so forth. Minton then asked if there was anything else. "Yes sir," I answered, "when Mr. Erwin sat on the bench at the booking desk, he fell off to the floor." Minton was sharp. He came back with, "Officer, would you say that bench is small for a man of Mr. Erwin's stature?" I stated, "I've never seen a sober man fall off of it." That got quite a bit of laughter from the courtroom.

"Ernie," Minton continued, "when we were talking some time back, you were telling me about a DWI arrest you had made that you wished you hadn't made and that lady you arrested turned out to not be drunk. Do you think you made the same mistake with Mr. Erwin?" I stated that I did not make a mistake–Erwin was drunk.

As for that lady I had told Minton about during my deposition, I noted that her blood test came back to show 0.06 percent blood alcohol when state law set 0.10 percent as the legal threshold of intoxication. I said that did not mean she wasn't too intoxicated to drive; just that she didn't meet the legal point of intoxication.

I could have given better testimony. The chancellor was a very personable guy and had not complained about anything when arrested. I also knew that in getting me to talk about those two old DWI cases, Minton had planted the thought in the minds of the jurors that I could have made a mistake with Erwin.

I was right. The jury was out about three hours before returning with a "not guilty" verdict. I was glad it came out that way for Erwin, but I also learned from that case to keep my mouth shut and only answer questions asked while doing a deposition.

Final Services for Lyndon B. Johnson

On January 22, 1973, the Secret Service contacted APD and requested assistance for the funeral of President Johnson who had died of a heart attack he suffered on his ranch near Johnson City. Most of the department was involved in the service which brought dignitaries from all over the world to Austin and Central Texas.

A few days before the services, as sergeant of the motorcycle shift that would handle the escort duties, I met with a 5th Army Colonel and the Secret Service.

Ernie Hinkle

At noon on January 23rd, we escorted Johnson's body from Weed-Corley Funeral Home at 3125 N. Lamar then to the LBJ Library. He lay in state there until 8 a.m. the following day. Then we escorted the body to Bergstrom Air Force Base for a flight to Washington, D. C. where he would lie in state in the rotunda of the Capitol.

Following a funeral service in Washington on January 25th, the President's body was returned to Texas for burial that afternoon.

Our motorcycle unit stayed busy handling traffic and escorts during this period when the whole world had its eyes on Central Texas. We all liked President Johnson and felt it was a privilege to serve in this way. On the day of the funeral, we escorted Mayor Roy Butler and the city council to Stonewall. I later received a letter from Lady Bird Johnson thanking us for our assistance through those last days of farewell.

Stonewall, Texas

February 14, 1973

Dear Sergeant Henkel:

Thank you for your support and
assistance through these last days
of farewell. Your personal help
in making events run smoothly contributed greatly during a trying
period.

Sincerely,

Lady Bird Johnson

Ernie Hinkle

Burglars Caught–Pickax Still in Door

In another case involving Officer Al Shaffer, I backed him up on a burglary call at Levines Department Store, 2735 East 7th Street. I arrived about 1:30 a.m. and saw Shaffer's police car in front of the building with no one around.

I went to the back of the store and noticed a pickax still in the door. About that time, I heard a shot. It sounded like it was about a block away. I headed that way and met Shaffer as he was coming back to the scene with three subjects in custody. He was soaking wet. He told me he had come up on them as they were trying to break open the back door of the department store with a pickax. When they ran, he chased them. He was gaining on them when he fell into some high water. About to lose the suspects, he fired a warning shot into the ground and they stopped. Shaffer was hard working and one of the most decorated officers on the force.

Protest in a Tree

Most of the protests we handled had to do with the ongoing war in Vietnam, but we responded to one situation in the 2400 block of San Jacinto Street involving a tree.

UT was expanding Memorial Stadium and a large oak tree needed to be removed. Some students objected to that, so seven of them climbed up the tree and would not come down. After three days, our department was called to get them out of the tree since it was delaying the project. The university had a district court injunction to get them moved.

Capt. Buddy Fann called me to the scene. The Fire Department was there with a hook and ladder truck. The captain looked at me and said, "Ernie, get them out of there." AFD had said it was the Police Department's responsibility. I don't like heights and didn't feel real good about doing any tree climbing. My motorcycle squad was with me and Officer Al Shaffer came over and said, "Ernie, I don't mind heights at all—I'll go up that tree and get them out."

I followed him up the ladder to where the limbs branched out. It was a huge tree. Four of the protestors came out of the tree and down the ladder, but the three others went up in the tree as far as they could. Shaffer pulled two of them down the tree to where I was standing at the tip of the ladder.

The last protestor, a female, went as high as she could up the tree, hanging out on a small limb. Shaffer reached her leg and was pulling on her when the limb broke. Fortunately, he was able to grab her by her arm. But now she was just hanging in midair. Shaffer assured her that he had her and told her to climb over him to a larger branch. She did as he instructed and then started climbing down to where I was. I assisted her to the ladder. She had an awful odor as she had lost control of her bowels.

Shaffer did a great job. When he caught the female in midair, he cracked three ribs and was in a lot of pain. He never complained–just did what he had to do, probably saving her life and maybe mine, too. Climbing trees was something we just didn't train to do. It was unusual, to say the least.

Officer's Gas Mask Not Working

During another anti-war protest, the crowd had moved in-to the street at 19th and Guadalupe.

I instructed the motorcycle shift to meet me at 19th and Whitis Avenue. I also called for the teargas and gas masks. We met the crowd head on and started throwing the gas grenades. As the gas started taking effect, the crowd broke up and went in all directions. I observed an officer down on his knees and went to him. He had the mask on, but couldn't breathe – he had forgotten to pull the plug off the filter. I pulled it off and Sgt. Mark Cutler coughed and then began to breathe fresh air again.

By now, the gas had thinned out of the air and we didn't need our masks anymore. Mark looked at me with my mask off and yanked his off. After a few deep breaths he said, "Hinkle, I

Ernie Hinkle

have been holding my breath." After he got his mask off we
had a good laugh about it.

I told Mark the same thing had happened to me before.
Most of the time we gassed ourselves before we could get our
masks on, especially during those times when we would get
overrun. We would use teargas only when a show of force
didn't work.

Held at Bay with Bow and Arrows

Officer David Huebel responded to a "nature unknown"
call at a residence on Hearn Street. On arrival, he was met at
the door by a woman who said her husband had gone crazy.
Then Huebel saw the man walking toward him with a rifle.
Huebel started backing out of the yard as he tried to talk the
man into laying the weapon down. Huebel made it to his patrol
car, backed out of the driveway and across the street and called
for backup.

I received the call about 12:40 p.m. on Aug. 30, 1971. By
the time I got there along with several other officers, the man
had exchanged his rifle for a bow and arrows. I was across the
street from the house with a vehicle parked at the curb between
me and the porch. I asked the man if I could cross the street
and talk with him. "Come ahead," he answered. I got about
halfway across and he said, "Leave your gun with someone
else."

Several officers had surrounded the house and I felt like
they had my back, so I gave my handgun to another officer. I
went across the street to the parked car. The man was now on
the other side of that vehicle with a drawn arrow pointed at me.
I started talking with him and his wife came over and joined
the conversation. We talked for several minutes before the man
saw Sgt. Albert Riley approaching the back of the car and ordered him to take his gun off, too. As Riley started taking his
gun off, the man's wife grabbed the arrow in the bow. I went
over the car, knocked him down, and Riley and I fought him

[96]

until we could get the cuffs on him. He went to jail pending a mental examination.

Without his wife's intervention, this incident could have ended very differently, especially for me, since I didn't have a protective vest on.

Street Vendor Gets His Wish

During the early 1970s, there were a lot of sidewalk sales along the Drag in the UT area from the 2200 through 2300 blocks of Guadalupe on the west side. The businesses in that area started to complain that the public couldn't get into their shops. As a result, the city council passed a new ordinance banning sidewalk sales. The ordinance had a 30-day grace period.

During that time, other officers and I who worked that area would walk through warning the street vendors to please move and handing out copies of the new ordinance. After the grace period ended, one person refused to move and proceeded to tell me "where I could go." He was sitting on a towel selling books. I placed him under arrest. Officer James Walsh drove up and I placed the vendor in the unit, along with his books, for a trip to jail.

It was a shame he had to go to jail to test the ordinance. But that ended selling on the sidewalk for a long time after that.

"Fired" over Dog Show

During the time I was on the motorcycle unit, we kept the motors at our homes. On my street, which ended in a cul-de-sac, we had six or seven children in the eight-to-ten-year-old range living around us. I would take them for rides along our street on my three-wheeler and got to be quite popular with them, giving them stick-on "Police Pal" badges and otherwise trying to show them that police officers are good guys.

Ernie Hinkle

Soon we had a neighborhood police force and the kids elected me chief. We would have regular meetings, mostly so they could take rides with me. They would tell me all kinds of things, like who was playing in the street and whose pet got out. My neighbor was retired and walked his boxer on a leash every day. My young "officers" would tell me whose yard the boxer had pooped on and that my neighbor hadn't cleaned it up.

All was well until the kids decided to have a pet parade. They elected me to escort the parade down our one-block street and then select the prettiest pet. The procession included four dogs, two cats, a rabbit, and a hamster. My neighbor had his boxer. All pets were on leashes or being carried. We went down Northwest Drive one block to the boxer owner's house to judge the pets. I must have been crazy to let myself be the animal judge. I thought I had an out, though. I picked the boxer to be first, but pointed out something special about each of the other animals. But that didn't work very well.

Everyone but my neighbor, the boxer owner, got mad at me. The sad-faced kids gathered up their pets and left. Later that day two little boys came by my house and told me I was no longer their chief. They were going to have a new good one. I told them I was very sorry and asked if I could still take them for a ride on the motorcycle. They said that would be okay.

I might add that my daughter had her cat, Tye, in the contest, too. That didn't go well for me, either.

Damage to City Property—Chief's Car

Chief Miles lived just around the corner from our house on Lazy Lane. It was a dead-end street with the only traffic being the residents who lived there. As the boys in our neighborhood grew up, they were always playing football in the street in front of the chief's house. That's where he parked his unmarked police car.

One day the boys were playing football in front of his house when they suddenly scattered. In just a little while, my son Ricky was knocking on the chief's door. Ricky told the

[98]

chief that a football had hit his car and broke the rear view mirror. Ricky gave the chief $2.25 to get it fixed and then left. A short time later, Ricky went back and told the chief that if there was money left over after fixing the mirror, to please call him and he would come get it. The chief said he told Ricky the amount he gave him would be about right to fix it.

I asked Ricky about it and he said, "Dad, when the ball hit his car, we all ran. I gathered all the guys up and we took up a collection to fix the mirror." That is my son. I am so very proud of him.

Fuzz ~ Pig

Sometime in the late 1960s when Ricky was about 10, he came home from Wooten Elementary School very upset. He said some people at school were calling me "Fuzz" and "Pig." I asked Ricky to feel my face and see if it felt fuzzy. He said, "No." I said, "See, they are not talking about Dad, and a pig is a smart animal so I am okay with that." After that, the name-calling didn't seem to bother him anymore.

During the Vietnam War demonstrations, protestors would often call the police "Fuzz" and "Pigs." It never bothered me. What did bother me was when they spat on us.

Suicides

You cannot work the streets as a police officer for 35 years without being involved in suicide or attempted suicide cases.

On January 25, 1972, about 1:30 p.m., I heard an officer call for an ambulance to meet him in the 1200 block of 45th Street where a man was threatening to shoot himself. I went to the scene and talked to Officer David Meredith who said that a person who lived there told him his roommate was talking about killing himself. I knocked on the apartment door but got no answer. After about the third knock I asked, "Sir, can I come

Ernie Hinkle

in? I am Ernie Hinkle with the Austin Police Department." He answered, "Come on in—the door is unlocked."

As I went in, he was sitting at the kitchen table holding a cocked .22 caliber pistol to his temple. He said, "Don't come any closer." I said, "Sir, I won't. I am afraid of you and I want to go home to my family tonight." I stood there and talked to him. Then, with his finger on the trigger, he pointed the gun at his left eye. I asked him if he believed in God. He answered that he sure did. I asked him to just look out of the window and see what a beautiful day it was. I tried to stress the basics of life and asked if he would like to take a walk in the greenbelt behind his apartment. Then I asked if I could sit down and he said okay.

Now he was holding the gun under his chin, finger still on the trigger. I said, "We have all got problems and it doesn't take long to see there are other problems bigger than our own." I said, "Sir, all I am asking for is the opportunity to get help for you." He said, "I don't know. I've made a decision today." I said, "It would be a big decision to just lay the gun down. I am scared as hell." He then asked, "Do you think I am not?" I said, "We are both scared." Then he said, "I need someone to talk to." I said, "I always have God to talk to. I put God first, others second, and me third."

He asked me if he would go to jail for threatening to kill himself. I told him he wouldn't go to jail, but that I would help him get someone to talk about his problems. At this point, I asked him if I could have the gun. He then asked me what it was like to be a police officer. I said, "I liked my job. It is out-side working with good people like you." He then un-cocked the gun and handed it to me. We went outside with arms around each other. Then I took him to the Police Department where the crisis team met us.

That was a good day for God, that young man, and me.

RESOLUTION

WHEREAS, Sgt. Ernie Hinkle has demonstrated the high professional standards for law enforcement officers everywhere, and has distinguished himself and his department in an outstanding manner while saving another's life; and

WHEREAS, Sgt. Hinkle, on January 25, 1972, set an example for sympathy, understanding and a high regard for another, when he entered an unknown situation, and convinced a despondent man to lay aside a weapon and submit to medical care; and

WHEREAS, Sgt. Hinkle placed himself third, after God and another person, during the tense confrontation, and his actions on that day typify the highest calling and greatest opportunity for a law enforcement officer to exhibit his special skills in the protection of human life; and

WHEREAS, in his eleven years as an Austin police officer, Sgt. Hinkle has twice helped residents from tragedy; on another occasion he convinced a man not to leap to death from the Congress Avenue Bridge;

NOW, THEREFORE, BE IT RESOLVED BY THE CITY COUNCIL OF AUSTIN, TEXAS:

That the City Council of the City of Austin hereby honors and recognizes the outstanding effort and dedication on the part of this law enforcement officer, and that a page be especially set apart in the Official Minutes of the City Council to recognize his brave actions, and that a copy of this resolution be presented to Sgt. Ernie Hinkle.

WITNESS OUR HANDS and the official Seal of the City of Austin, Texas, this the 17th day of February, 1972.

ATTEST:

Mayor

Mayor Pro Tem

Councilman

Councilman

Councilman

Councilman

Councilman

City Clerk

Embarrassment on the Stand

One of my more embarrassing moments as an officer came when I was waiting to testify in district court. The courtroom was packed. When I was called to the stand and after being sworn in, the judge told me to have a seat. As I sat down, the backside of my uniform pants ripped from top to bottom. You could hear it all over the courtroom followed by some laughter.

District Judge Mace B. Thurman called court to order and then asked, "Officer, do you have a problem?" "Yes, sir," I said. He said after my testimony he would follow me to his chambers to discuss it. When that happened, he shielded my exposed butt from view. Judge Thurman was a great judge.

Humor in the Courtroom

Officer Doyne Bailey had a burglary case in Judge Thurman's court. The judge called the defendant to the bench and asked how he wanted to plead. When the man entered a plea of guilty, Thurman pronounced the sentence.

"Sir," he said, "this is the sixth time you have been in my court. I sentence you to 90 years in the penitentiary." Obviously not expecting that, the shocked defendant said, "Judge, I won't live that long." The judge looked at him for a moment and said, in a kindly way, "Just try and do the best you can."

Hard-Working and Fun-Loving

Our platoon was a hard-working, fun-loving group of officers. They were dedicated to their jobs protecting the citizens of Austin; but, along the way, there was always room to jack with each other.

In the 1960s, there was a poultry market across the street from the police station, El East Poultry and Market. Live

[102]

chickens came in nightly by the truckloads. They were always getting out of the cages and running all over the area. For fun, officers occasionally chased down a chicken and put it in someone's unit. I ran several chickens out of my vehicle. It didn't make any difference whether my unit was locked. Somehow, officers would find a way to get in my unit and leave me a chicken. In addition to chickens, I have removed armadillos, rabbits, ducks, and other critters from my unit.

One evening on arriving home from work, I found a "For Sale" sign in our yard. Another time someone, I'm sure a fellow officer, listed my pickup truck "For Sale" in the newspaper. I had numerous calls on it and could have sold it if I had wanted to, which I didn't.

I never minded those kinds of pranks too much. A little humor is a good thing, especially in something as serious as police work.

Close to Shooting a Wino

We referred to a person living on the streets, always drinking, eating out of garbage cans, and bumming money anyway they could get it, as winos. Not as politically correct as "homeless people," but that's what we called them – winos. At that time, most of them were there because they wanted to be there. I tried to help them, but most of them just didn't seem to want to change the way they lived.

Over time, I got to know a lot of them. They seemed to have loyalty between themselves and would very seldom fight each other. One Friday about midnight, a call went out to check on a suspicious person in the north alley of 700 East 6th Street. I was about two blocks away. I turned my lights off as I entered the alley and got out of my unit. The alley was pitch-dark. As I started walking, I could see and hear someone in front of me.

I said, "Police! Stop where you are!" The light from my flashlight caught a glimpse of a subject holding a gun on me. I told him to drop the gun. He stated he was going to kill me. I drew my weapon and we had a standoff. I began to walk closer.

"I am going to shoot you," he said. But before he could do that, I had gotten close enough to him to knock the gun out of his hand with my nightstick. When I did that, he took off running with me close behind. I hit him again with my nightstick and he went down. I cuffed him and then called for an ambulance. At about this time I recognized him as a local wino.

I went back and found the gun. Back in my car, I discovered his "weapon" was just a toy pistol. But it had sure looked real when he was holding it on me.

I picked him up at Brackenridge ER after he had his head sewn up and booked him into jail for "drunk." He didn't know how close he had come to getting shot that night. I know God was riding with us on many occasions.

Actual Toy Gun Used by Wino.

Winter Tragedy

At times during freezing weather, I would drive the alleys along the lower west side of Congress Avenue. Street people would crawl up under the buildings to sleep. They would sleep on cardboard or cover themselves with cardboard to try to stay warm and dry. I tried getting them to go to the Salvation Army for the night, but most of them would tell me to "Get lost." I don't know how they could handle the freezing weather—they were tough people.

One night I was patrolling the downtown area and saw a city street sweeper parked and unattended in the 100 block of East 4th Street on the north curb. I came back by about two hours later and saw what looked like a body lying next to the curb at about the same place the street sweeper had been parked. Stopping for a closer look, I saw it was definitely a body with a piece of cardboard over his head. I pulled the cardboard back and saw that his head had been run over. It wasn't a pretty picture.

I called for the medical examiner and started an investigation. We found the street sweeper and asked the driver to come back to the scene. When I talked with him, he said he had stopped to eat and had been out of service for about an hour. While the sweeper had been parked, a wino had crawled under it and gone to sleep. The driver of the sweeper had no idea someone was under the heavy city vehicle when he started it up and drove off. He never saw him or knew he was under the sweeper. The right rear tire tread perfectly matched the tracks on the cardboard that had been covering the man's head. Sadly, he had chosen the wrong place to go to sleep.

LIEUTENANT

Promotion to Lieutenant

In 1973, I decided to take the test for promotion to lieutenant. I had been studying some, but not seriously. I enjoyed the motorcycle shift and worked with a great bunch of officers. We had gone through several active years handling numerous anti-war demonstrations that got out of hand.

Remembering how hard I had to work to make sergeant and knowing I still wasn't a very good test taker, I started studying diligently. I took the test during the first part of the year and passed, making lieutenant on June 24, 1973.

By then, I had a pretty good idea of the kind of officer I wanted working for me. This is what I looked for: First, a people person with a good attitude, an officer who could resolve the problem at hand without involving criminal law. Second, I wanted honesty, loyalty, and integrity. Sir Robert Peel (considered the father of police procedures in England and America), defines police service as "making a low number of arrests while still accomplishing compliance with the law." That's how I tried to do my job, and that's what I looked for in the officers who reported to me.

One of the Best Memos I Ever Received

As I was in the process of being transferred off of the midnight and motorcycle shift and being promoted to lieutenant, the officers I worked with presented me with this memo. What a great group of officers! This is the best memo I ever received:

Ernie Hinkle

MEMO TO:ALL OFFICERS

SUBJECT: ASSIGNMENT OF PERSONNEL TO 4pm-12am SHIFT

THE 4PM TO 12AM MIDNIGHT SHIFT WILL BE COMPOSED OF THE FOLLOWING:

PERSONNEL:

ONE SERGEANT (ERNIE HINKLE #317) AND SIXTEEN PATROLMEN (
HOWARD PARK,DELBERT MCCULLOUGH,HAROLD RIGBY,ALBERT RILEY,VERNON STEHLING,
JOHN STONE, JOHN ROSS, HARRY EASTMAN, CLAUDE HILL, ROBERT HARGIS, JOHN
BRANTLEY, JAMES COONEY, JUSTIN SHAFFER, JAMES FRENZEL) ASSIGNED TO TEN
DISTRICTS. FIVE OF THE SIXTEEN PATROLMEN WILL BE ASSIGNED TO RELIEF SHIFTS
AND TEN WILL BE ASSIGNED TO REGULAR DISTRICTS. THE COMPLETE SHIFT, ONE
SERGEANT AND SIXTEEN PATROLMEN, WILL ROTATE EACH 28 DAYS FROM THE 4-12
SHIFT TO THE MOTORCYCLE SHIFT. THE MOTORCYCLE SHIFT WILL THEN WORK 4-12
FOR 28 DAYS.

THIS SHIFT LATER BEEFED UP WITH LEONARD SNYDER, JACK LEO, JAMES
BAKER,ROOSEVELT SAMPSON,ERNEST SHUGART, DARRELL GAMBRELL,MIKE SLATER,
EMZIE ECKERT,JOHN WOLBRUECK, JOHN TAYLOR, LOUIE WHITE, AND COY WEBER
WERE TO SET ALL KINDS OF RECORDS IN THE FOLLOWING TWO YEARS AND THREE
MONTHS. NO GROUP OF POLICEMEN,WORKING TOGETHER,HAVE EVER BEEN HELD
TOGETHER AS A TEAM BY A MORE OUTSTANDING LEADER. THE MOST OUTSTANDING
SHIFT OF POLICEMEN EVER ORGANIZED WISHES TO SAY

THANK YOU

My First Assignment as a Lieutenant

Shortly after I made lieutenant, Chief Miles called me to his office and told me he was establishing a new community relations program. He wanted to establish two storefronts—one at 7th Street and Canadian, and one on Montopolis Drive. He said Capt. Harland Moore would be over the program and added that he wanted me to work that program for at least a year.

The chief knew I wanted to stay on the street, but I was willing to do it.

In 1973, the department had three patrol platoons, each with 50 to 55 officers. These officers covered five sectors with a sergeant and ten officers in each. Sectors were broken down into eight to ten districts. In addition, the department had a Criminal Investigation Division made up of detectives who investigated the seven major crimes: Homicide, rape, robbery, burglary, theft, auto theft, and forgery. Officers would start an investigation on the street and then turn it over to the detectives to follow-up. The Service Division was responsible for training, recruiting, building maintenance, vehicles, supplies, and the pistol range.

The year I made lieutenant, APD investigated 26 murders, 16 negligent homicides, 90 rapes, 309 robberies, 978 aggravated assaults, 4,462 burglaries, 9,625 thefts, 1,066 auto thefts, and 939 other assaults for a total of 17,511 actual offenses reported.

In creating the community relations program, the Chief's goal was to be more proactive with our citizens. In most cases, the only contact with citizens by the police came in responding to a call. Again, our aim was to go out into the public and make as many personal contacts as possible. Also assigned to this unit were Sgts. Ray Sanders and Roosevelt Sampson, Officers Dan Richards, Billy Sifuentes and James New, and two police aides.

We started walking areas around the two storefronts, both of which were in high-call areas. We would leave people crime prevention pamphlets with an invitation for them to come by the storefronts to visit us. We also went to all the schools and churches in those areas. I made all the Show-ups at the police station to urge officers to get out of their units and meet the people in their districts anytime they had a chance to do so. That was asking a lot, because in those days district officers stayed pretty busy responding to calls. We were usually short-handed and, if someone was on vacation or out sick, it would cut manpower down to five or six officers to cover a sector.

Sgt. Sanders began contacting businesses in the down-town area in an effort to see how the department could better serve them. He distributed handouts on crime prevention and the merchants seemed to appreciate it.

We also contacted most of the car dealerships to work on ways to better secure their car lots and prevent vehicle theft. We also reached out to apartment rental managers to set up meetings with their residents to go over crime prevention pro-grams. As hard as it is to believe, many apartment dwellers don't lock their doors nor do they have an escape plan in case of a fire.

Finally, we started a crime prevention home inspection program. It's hard to measure success in a program like this, but I like to think we prevented some crimes from happening.

Blue Santa

During our crime prevention contacts, which mostly were on the east side, we discovered several older people and some single parents with children who wouldn't have much for Christmas. In October 1974, we were sitting around the office trying to think of some kind of Christmas program the depart-ment could support. What we came up with was a decision to seek donations to give Christmas gifts and food to needy fami-lies for Christmas.

Now we had to decide what we were going to call the program. We bounced several names around before Sgt. Sand-ers said, "Well, we have blue uniforms, let's call it Blue Santa." That name stuck and the program is still going strong. Sanders went on to become assistant chief. Now retired, he was a great leader.

I went to the Police Association about the program and they donated $150 to get it started. The Austin American-Statesman published an article and we began to get donations from citizens, Safeway, UT Silver Spurs, the Boy Scouts and other businesses and organizations. We received several mail-in contributions, as well.

That Christmas Eve, we delivered around 85 Christmas packages. El East Produce Co. donated a hen for each family. The next year, 1975, officers sent us information about needy families in their districts. We learned from our experiences in the first year of the gift-giving program how to better manage it. For one thing, it was too difficult to deliver to families on Christmas Eve, so we switched to doing it three days before Christmas. Blue Santa also started working with the Christmas Bureau, then headed by Mae Waggoner.

The second year of the program, ten officers delivered food and gifts to 142 needy families representing about 600 recipients. Earlier that year, the department put on a Blue Santa Bowl football game to raise funds. We ended up with a surplus of supplies and were able to help the Christmas Bureau with 45 additional families.

One Blue Santa donation was very heart-warming. An elderly man drove up to the police storefront at 7th and Canadian Streets in an old Model "T" truck. He had five live chickens in a coop and wanted to give them to needy families. "I don't have much to give," he said, "but these chickens can make five families a dinner." You could tell he was a poor man, but to me he was the richest man I would ever know. The donor did want his coop back after we gave the chickens away. The birds went to families on Webberville Road who said they would have them for a Christmas dinner.

The Blue Santa program has continued to grow over the years, making Christmas special for many people, including the officers who make it happen. Because of this and other things we did, I enjoyed the community relations work. Meeting our citizens on a different level showed me a different side of police work that was very rewarding—the public getting to know the police officer as a person, not just a blue uniform.

Back to Patrol

About a year to 18 months after I became a lieutenant, Chief Miles called me to his office again and said he was going to fulfill the promise he made me when he assigned me to the community policing unit – I could go back to a patrol shift. Really happy to get back on the street, I was assigned to Capt. Gerald Spohnholtz's platoon.

I started out on the night shift from 11 p.m. to 7 a.m. I found out soon I had a lot to learn after being off the street for more than a year and, before then, in motorcycles for five years. Officers were making their calls, but I didn't think the sergeants were on top of what was going on in their sectors. To improve that, I started working one sector at a time, making back-up calls. I really worked my butt off. If the sergeant didn't show up, I would call to see what they were doing. I wasn't very popular for a while, but I felt the sergeants should be leaders, not just supervisors.

Another thing I noticed was that there was very little lateral communication between the sectors. I called a meeting with all the sergeants and suggested they lighten up and have some fun while doing their jobs. I addressed the problem of officers bypassing their sergeants and coming directly to me by sending them back to their sergeants. It was hard to do sometimes, but it was the right thing to do. After about four or five months, things got better.

We changed shifts every 28 days. At shift change, we would have a barbeque or go on a fishing trip to Capt. Spohnholtz's lake house at Sunrise Beach.

One time our entire platoon went deep-sea fishing. Sgt. Robert Dahlstrom (David Sector supervisor) planned our fishing trip and chartered a boat out of Rockport. Robert worked hard collecting the money for chartering the boat and making the arrangements for the trip. A great person, he retired as an assistant chief. After retirement, he became chief of the UT Police Department until his retirement in 2013. It takes a special person to accomplish that level of achievement.

Getting back to our expedition, that trip turned out to be quite a mess. A lot of the guys partied pretty hard the night we got there. About half of them got sick the next morning just going across the bay to get to our chartered boat. The weather couldn't have been worse—we had high waves and rough water. By the time the charter boat captain got where he wanted to fish, all 55 of us were sick. Most of the officers were lying in beds in the bunkroom, with others scattered around the deck. I think Assistant Chief George Phifer was about the only one not throwing up, and he wasn't moving around much himself. Incidentally, he was a good chief—very smart and dedicated.

I remember Officer Wayne Simer was holding on to the boat railing so sick he wanted somebody to just shoot him. Wayne was one of the finest officers I was privileged to work with.

Finally, I asked the boat captain to take us back to land. I don't remember any fish being caught. It was a sad-looking bunch of guys by the time we got back to the dock. That was the last time we ever went deep-sea fishing as a group.

But our platoon really bonded. We were a team that usually led the department in activity and had the fewest complaints. We were a hard-working, dedicated, fun-loving group of officers.

We got the first female officer on our platoon in 1976, Penny Hubert. I was somewhat worried about it since it would be something new for me, for her and the department. At first, she seemed to fit in really well, and then she was involved in a bad collision in a police vehicle. She was okay, but it seemed to set her back. She was well accepted and doing a good job, but she didn't stay with the department long.

I don't know why I was ever concerned about female officers. Over the years, I was lucky to be able to work with some outstanding women cops. They fit well in the police profession and were a definite asset to my platoon.

Once I received some complaints about Officer Karen Alexander spending too much time at the police station. She was working Baker Sector downtown, which covered the area around headquarters. I ran into Karen leaving the Show-down room about 2 o'clock one morning.

"Karen, I hear you are spending a lot of time here at the station," I said. Boy, did I get a direct answer.

"Lieutenant," she said, "I stop by here to pee. I just can't whip it out like you do. I have to take all this stuff off and the station is in my district."

I said, "Karen, you spend as much time here at the station as you want to. I am sorry I said anything."

A woman's bathroom needs was something we men never thought about. Karen was an outstanding officer, very responsible. I am a better person for having known her. Her husband, Bill, was also a police officer.

Small Task Force – Big Impact!

In early September 1986, Sgt. Jerry Staton, the facilitator on our platoon, talked to me about forming a small task force within our Platoon III. A facilitator (in this case) is a police sergeant in street clothes. One facilitator would be assigned to each platoon to conduct assignments that, normally, a uniformed officer could not do. Sgt. Staton was a great communicator and an excellent teacher. He was always thinking out of the box on ways to catch criminals. I thought it was a great idea.

We now had six sectors on our platoon with approximately ten officers and one senior sergeant on each sector. To pull one officer off of each sector would put a heavy load on the other officers, especially if an officer was on vacation, sick leave, etc. In talking it over with our platoon, all the officers thought it was a good idea. We would work harder to make it work.

With my platoon's approval, we presented it to our Shift Commander, Capt. John Vasquez. Capt. Vasquez wanted us to pull the task force together as soon as we could. He advised me he would support us in any way he could.

Sgt. Staton went to each sector soliciting volunteers for his task force. The following officers were selected: Bruce Lutringer, Mark Gilcrest, Mark Payne, Doug Ross, M. Fuentes, and D. Funderburgh. What a great success it turned out to be! These officers working together as a team performed a great police service busting street drug dealers, arresting persons who had a large number of traffic and felony warrants, doing surveillance for robberies and auto theft, etc.

This following case is just one example of the success of the task force. We had been having a rash of residential burglaries in northwest Austin. The suspect was identified, but we couldn't locate him. I talked to Sgt. Keith Burt in the Crime Analysis Unit and he sent out a wanted bulletin and updated information on Jerome D. Chaney's mode of operation.

Ernie Hinkle

Wanted

Persons

Bulletin

CONFIDENTIAL: FOR POLICE USE ONLY

DATE ISSUED: <u>October 24, 1986</u>

ISSUED BY: <u>M. Rech #403</u>

RESIDENTIAL BURGLAR
"NORTHWEST AUSTIN DOOR KICKER"

WARRANTS HAVE BEEN ISSUED ON THE NORTHWEST AUSTIN RESIDENTIAL BURGLAR WHOSE M.O. HAS BEEN FORCING THE FRONT DOOR AND TAKING JEWELRY AND HANDGUNS.

WANTED * * * * * WANTED * * * * * WANTED * * * * * WANTED * * * * * WANTED

JEROME D. CHANEY
WHITE MALE, 11-17-41
AKA: ROLAND FORREST, GERALD ASHLEY, ROBERT FULTON
LKA: 803 RANCH ROAD, GEORGETOWN, TEXAS

VEHICLES

BROWN 75 FORD GRANADA - 86 TX. 281 NAP
MAROON 79 PONTIAC 2DR. - 86 TX. 352 MMV
WHITE/MAROON 74 BUICK 2DR. - 86 TX. JXR 725

WARRANTS ISSUED

1.   BURGLARY/HABITATION - 1ST DEGREE FELONY - #153948 - $15,000 BOND
2.   BURGLARY/HABITATION - BOND FORFEITURE - 331ST DISTRICT COURT - NO BOND SET

CHANEY MAY BE IN THE COMPANY OF ASSOCIATES THAT ARE ALSO COMMITTING BURGLARIES. ALL OCCUPANTS OF THE ABOVE VEHICLES SHOULD BE CONSIDERED **ARMED AND DANGEROUS**. CHANEY IS A DRUG ADDICT AND HAS STOLEN SEVERAL PISTOLS IN BURGLARIES. CHANEY MAY ALSO HAVE A SMALL PRYBAR OR SIMILAR ITEM IN HIS POSSESSION THAT SHOULD BE TAGGED AS EVIDENCE. SEE PHOTO ON BACK.

IF MORE INFORMATION IS NEEDED, CONTACT SGT. KEITH BURT (EXT. 5130) OR CRIME ANALYSIS - MIKE RECH (EXT. 5265).

PREPARED BY CRIME ANALYSIS - MR/sar
RESTRICTED DISTRIBUTION - POLICE INFORMATION

CRIME ANALYSIS UNIT	BULLETIN # 1008	FORM #

Sgt. Staton put his task force on this case and, within 24 hours, Jerome Chaney was arrested in the north alley of the 1100 block of East 12th Street at 10:30 am. trying to buy drugs.

I could write so much more about the work the task force performed; however, Deputy Chief Don Doyle of the Criminal Investigations Bureau pretty much summed it up in a commendation letter to Sgt. Staton and each of the six officers on the task force. Reading the memo below will give you insight on only one of many great things that came from the task force. Chief Don Doyle was not one to hand out many commendations—he just expected everyone to do their jobs. That is why this memo is so special:

Ernie Hinkle

M E M O R A N D U M

TO: CAPTAIN JOHN VASQUEZ

FROM: D. DOYLE, DEPUTY CHIEF

DATE: OCTOBER 29, 1986

SUBJECT: COMMENDATION - ARRESTS

Some weeks ago, your platoon began forming small task forces to work on special projects. These, to my knowledge, included a concentrated effort to arrest persons on whom we held a large number of traffic warrants, busting street drug dealers, and doing surveillance on auto thieves. These efforts have resulted in a number of good arrests, each one chipping a little bit off the crime rate, and giving the public a little more protection for their property and persons.

I am aware of no heroic deeds they have performed—just cops doing a good job, earning their pay, showing citizens they care, and going home at the end of their day knowing they have done things cops need to do. On October 28th, Sgt. Staton's group, B. Lutringer, M. Fuentes, M. Gilchrest, D. Funderberg, M. Payne and D. Ross, under the direction of Lt. Hinkle, arrested Jerome Chaney, a habitual criminal and very active burglar.

Chaney's arrest will clear a large number of resident burglaries. This is good—but much better and more important is the fact that there are perhaps hundreds of Austin citizens who will not have their homes burglarized because your troops put Chaney in jail. These citizens do not know that this arrest has spared them the anger and frustration that all burglary victims feel, but we know it, and commend all the troops involved.

D. Doyle, Deputy Chief
Criminal Investigation Bureau

DD/cm

[120]

Losing a Friend Hurts

In January 1976, working the night shift, I heard a "nature unknown" call at the 7-Eleven Store at Koenig Lane and North Lamar.

Officer David Lysek soon arrived at the store and immediately called for an ambulance. I checked by and told David that I would follow up on the call at Brackenridge Hospital ER. At the hospital, I found a man in the waiting room who was extremely distressed and emotional. He told me that he and his best friend of many years had been on their way back to Austin from a fishing trip when his fishing buddy became very ill. He could tell his friend was in a bad way and had stopped at the convenience store to get help.

I told him I would see how his friend was doing and went back to the crash room. The doctor told me the man had been dead on arrival at the hospital.

Now I had the unpleasant task of telling the man in the waiting room that his best friend had died. This is something no police officer wants to do, but it comes with the territory. I went back and said, "Sir, your friend didn't make it." I added that I was very sorry and that I was there with him to help in any way I could. Naturally, he was very distraught. We sat and talked for a while as I tried to assure him that he had done all he could have possibly done for his friend.

Little did I realize that 28 years later, in 2004, I would lose my best friend and fishing partner in basically the same way. We spent a lot of time on the water together; but, for some reason, we had not gone bass fishing the previous week. Anytime we didn't see each other during the week, one or the other of us would call on Sunday mornings to check in. So about 8 o'clock on Sunday morning, I called. He didn't answer, so I left a message on his recorder teasing him that he needed to pick up the phone. Then my wife and I went to church.

When we returned home, we got a call from, Rita, the captain's wife, who said we had lost Gerald. He had a massive heart attack and passed away on the way to the hospital. What

[121]

a loss in our lives. When you have a friend you are always doing things with, not to mention our long law enforcement career together, a strong bond develops and you feel lost without him. I was blessed to have had a friend like Capt. Gerald Spohnholtz and I miss him so very much. I still do some bass fishing, but it's not the same without him.

I remembered a letter Chief Miles had forwarded to me from Mr. Raven in 1976. After losing my best friend, the letter took on a different meaning. I definitely know how he felt losing his best friend.

January 22, 1976

Mr. R. A. Miles, Chief of Police
Austin Police Department
700 East 7th
Austin, Texas   78701

Dear Chief Miles:

On January 18, I had the distressing experience of having my
closest friend, Virgil Weber, die on the way home from a fishing
trip.

By the time I reached Austin and realized that he was in a bad
way, I was panic-stricken. I pulled into a convenience store
to seek help (North Lamar at Koenig Lane). The nigh attendant
was helpful and called your Department.

The first officer that arrived took command of the situation
in a considerate and professional manner. I had no idea that
Law Enforcement officers could be so concerned for the feelings
of others.

After I arrived at the emergency section of Brackenridge Hospital,
a Lieutenant seemed to make it his responsibility to see that
every consideration was extended to me.

I have made a special effort to identify these two officers who,
to me, are very special. If they are representative of the
Austin Police Department, as I am sure they are, then you have
every reason to be proud to be the head of a superb organization.

The two men were:

> Officer: David Lysek
>
> Lieutenant: Ernie Hinkle

Please convey to them my sincere thanks.

Yours very truly,

H. O. Raven

HOR:dms

Ernie Hinkle

Uhhh, Hello Out There

I had a reputation for not always following procedure when it came to using my radio. That's something I am not proud of. But if I drove up on a situation in progress, I would usually jump out of my unit and get into the middle of it before I radioed what I was doing. You would think I would know better, but I got into trouble more than once by not letting the dispatcher know where I was.

One Saturday about 2 a.m., I drove up on a large fight at the Tequila Bar in the 1700 block of East 6th Street. I turned the overhead red lights on, pulled into the parking lot, and jumped out of my car to break up the fight. The parking lot was crowded with several people fighting. All of a sudden, the crowd turned on me.

I was in trouble having been backed up against a wall trying to talk myself out of there. About that time, I saw Sgt. Manuel "Mito" Peña drive up. He came out of his car with his shotgun in his hands, speaking Spanish. The crowd scattered like quail. Within ten minutes, the parking lot was empty.

Sgt. Peña (now a retired lieutenant) was one of the best and hardest-working officers I ever worked with. He was very special—not just because he saved my butt and possibly my life that night, but because he had the respect of all who knew him. Anyway, the next time I got out of my unit I used the radio first.

Another time, about midnight, I was in the eastbound lane at East 6th and Comal waiting for a red light to change. I noticed some people coming out of a bar across the street from Cisco's Bakery. As I watched, two men pulled guns and started shooting at each other right in front of me.

I put my unit in reverse and backed up about half a block. I saw one subject fall and the other take off running. I started chasing him in my unit until he cut down an alley. I bailed out of my car and started after him on foot. I saw him toss his gun and I caught him about a block away and cuffed him. On the way back to my unit, I found the gun he had tried to get rid of.

I put him in my unit and went back to where the shooting started, expecting to find a body.

But when I got back to the bar, not only was there no body, no one was around, either. The place was locked up and all the lights were off. I couldn't even find a drop of blood in the area.

Back at the station, I booked the shooter for discharging a firearm in the city limits, a misdemeanor. I figured that, sooner or later, a gunshot victim would show up at one of the hospitals, but no one did. The two guys had been shooting point blank at each other. It was incredible that somebody wasn't hit.

I also couldn't believe that, once again, I had forgotten to call in my location. And this time, I had been chasing a man with a gun in his hand.

Remember the early 1960s TV comedy, "Car 54, Where Are You?" Well, one Sunday night in May 1975 at APD, it was "Car 202, (my unit) Where Are You?" The dispatcher had repeatedly attempted to raise me on the radio. After about 45 minutes, they put out a search for me and my unit, Unit 202. One officer reported that he had seen me stopped on Ben White Boulevard talking to some subjects about the time the dispatcher started calling me. This information started an extensive search for me in South Austin.

What happened was that I was having car trouble and had taken the car to the police garage. I got preoccupied with getting my car fixed and wasn't listening to the radio. I left my unit at the garage and walked across the street to the captain's office. When he saw me walking in, Capt. Spohnholtz picked up the phone and called the dispatcher to cancel the lookout for me.

"Hinkle," he said, "you scared the crap out of us and next time that happens, whether you are in trouble or not, I am going to kick the 'you know what' out of you." That was that!

I felt really badly about what had happened. We had a close platoon and I believe I got a butt-chewing from all 65 officers at one point or another. Capt. Spohnholtz was a great person. He cared for the officers and was definitely a leader, not just a supervisor.

Well, it didn't stop there. The newspaper ran a story headlined "Car 202, Where Are You?" It was the talk of the police station, though I really didn't think it was that funny. In fact, it was probably one of the most embarrassing times of my career.

About a year later, I was working a demonstration at the LBJ Library. I was using the public address system in Unit 304, trying to talk people out of the street. We got the situation settled down and I went back on patrol. Unfortunately, I had forgotten to turn off the PA system.

Later, I discovered this memo from Sgt. Sam Warren posted on the bulletin board at headquarters:

> "Dear Lt. Ernie Hinkle,
> When you put on your shining armor and go out into the night to the UT area, even though we know you are the friend of the friendless, that you must speak to all the street vendors, hippies and rioters, you must remember instead of leaving a radio request for repair because your radio will not transmit, just turn the dial back to radio from PA."

I got the message—I had erroneously written up a repair request to have the radio fixed. It was my negligence that I left the PA system on and didn't turn it back to radio. It didn't take the repair technician long to fix it.

As for following radio procedure, after that I always tried to concentrate on using the radio before I went out on back-ups, traffic stops, or for anything else. I also tried to make sure that no one who worked on my shift ignored the radio. If an officer didn't answer the radio, I would usually pull him out of the unit and send him to the radio room for the day.

No Such Thing as a Routine Disturbance

On March 31, 1977, Officers Chris Walker and Harold Hoffmeister responded to a disturbance call at a mobile home park in the 6100 block of South Congress about 8:30 p.m. As Walker approached the trailer where the disturbance was coming from, an elderly man opened the door and shouted obscenities at the officer, then closed the door. Just a few minutes later, the man opened the door again and the officers saw he was armed with a pistol.

The officers took cover and tried to talk the man into dropping the weapon. Instead, he started shooting at the officers and then he went back into his trailer and closed the door.

As street lieutenant, I was notified of the shooting and responded to the scene. We again called to the man to come out and give up. Once again, he opened the door to the trailer in an attempt to shoot at the officers. However, this time we had officers on both sides of the door. As the door opened, they tackled the man and took him into custody without further incident.

As it turned out, the fellow was 84 years old and mad at the world. He was taken to city jail pending charges. The officers did a great job. This incident is a perfect example of what a police officer faces on a disturbance call. You never know what to expect. In this case, the man with the weapon was mad at society and took it out on the cops.

So often police officers are faced with a "shoot or don't shoot" situation. With their own lives on the line, the officers would have been justified in shooting back in this case. What would you have done?

Aggravated Assault – Murder

Show-up is a place where officers meet before going on duty to receive any updates and to learn of any new persons on the wanted list. On August 31, 1977, about five minutes into the 11 p.m. Show-up, Capt. R. G. Wilkes called me and said a person had barricaded himself in a residence in the 6900 block of Providence in East Austin and had wounded or shot one person in the house.

At that time, APD did not have a SWAT team. Street officers handled whatever came up and did a pretty good job of it. Believe me! I was glad when we finally did get a specialized unit to respond to these types of calls.

I arrived at the scene about 11:20 p.m. Once there, I met with Sgt. Larry Stanley, Officers Gary Barrington, David Lysek, Robert Hasselman, Daniel Pence, and others who had set up a perimeter around the area. We could hear gunshots from inside the house as Stanley briefed me. The sergeant said a woman who had run out of the house told officers her son had gone crazy, stabbed her husband (his father), beat him with a gun, and then started shooting everywhere. Now she feared her husband was dead.

She told us there was more than one gun in the house. Meanwhile, we could hear the man inside cursing and saying things like, "You ain't got no search warrant, you mother-@#&$ing pigs." He was screaming almost unintelligibly. In checking with our dispatcher, I learned the thirty-three-year-old man had an extensive record including three stays in the state prison in Huntsville where he had done about ten years.

I asked the dispatcher to call the residence, hoping I could talk to the guy. We could hear the phone ringing, but he didn't answer.

Officer Barrington said the man had briefly come out the back door, waving a pistol in his right hand. Barrington had a clear shot at him, but felt the man was trying to commit suicide by cop. As Barrington thought about that, the man ran back into the house and shot again.

We discussed our options. We had gas grenades, but I didn't want to use gas because of the injured person inside. I also didn't want to rush the house. There was too big a chance that we would get an officer shot.

It was a hot summer night and all the windows and doors were open. The house, which sat on a corner lot, was mostly dark with the exception of a room in the back. I talked with Sgt.

Stanley and told him I was going to move closer to the house. I said that until he heard from me, to keep all the officers under cover. Up until now, all the shooting had been inside the house, not toward us. I got on my unit's public address system and asked the guy inside if I could talk to him. He said, "Come on in." He was in the front part of the house, so I took off for the back door. Barrington followed me and took cover behind a vehicle.

When I made it to the back door, I peeped around the frame and could see a man lying in a pool of blood on the kitchen floor. I also saw a big man standing in a hallway leading from the kitchen. He was pointing a pistol at the back door in my general direction.

The kitchen door was ajar, but the screen door opened to the inside and a kitchen table had been pushed against it. I asked if I could come in and he said I could. Telling him I didn't want anyone to get hurt, I asked if he would put the gun down. He pointed the gun toward the back door and the weapon snapped and then snapped a second time. Thinking he was out of bullets, I went crashing through the screen door, got the gun from him and the fight was on. I called for help yelling, "He is unarmed." Before any of the other officers got inside, he picked me up and slammed me into a doorframe. I heard my shoulder crack and knew that I was injured, but did not know how badly until later.

By now, all the officers were struggling with him. He fought violently, like a crazy man. After much difficulty, we finally succeeded in cuffing him. An ambulance was already there and took his father to Brackenridge ER. The older man was still alive, but barely. We found flesh all over the kitchen floor where the father had been pistol-whipped. His upper lip was gone and his face looked like it had been run through a meat grinder.

All the officers involved in this incident did a great job. We worked as a team in an extremely dangerous situation without getting anyone killed, which was a blessing. We had several opportunities to shoot the man; and, as it turned out, I almost wish we had. Instead, he was booked in jail. You will better understand my thinking as you continue to read this case.

In my offense report, I wrote that I thought the defendant was a danger to society. He had told me that he had been in the Rusk State Hospital for the criminally insane. I didn't think he should be eligible to bond out of jail. He was freaking crazy.

The pistol we took as evidence that night went to our ballistics folks for examination. Someone from the lab later contacted me with sobering news. The suspect had pulled the trigger twice on empty chambers. I had heard both clicks since he was pointing the weapon at me. I had thought the gun was empty, but the next chamber held a live round. If he had dropped the hammer again, I probably would have been shot. I thank God for being with me that night.

I told Lt. Colon Jordan, who headed the homicide unit, that I considered Kenneth Felder to be the most dangerous person I had ever dealt with. Jordan followed up by having a Mental Health-Mental Retardation psychiatrist examine Felder. The doctor, who obviously did not see Felder the way I experienced him when we were trying to get him in custody that night, refused to recommend commitment.

The lieutenant found out Felder was under indictment on two counts of burglary and scheduled to be prosecuted as a habitual criminal. If Felder got "bitched," as crooks called a habitual conviction, he would get life in prison. Jordan sought a peace officer's commitment, but state mental hospitals would not accept prisoners with charges pending against them. Meanwhile, Felder was transferred to the Travis County Jail.

During a pre-trial hearing on burglary and habitual criminal charges, District Judge Mace B. Thurman set a high bond and Felder went back to jail. But a Municipal Court Judge reduced his bond to $5,000 and Felder was released on September 8th after posting bond through AAA Bonding Company.

Seven days after his release from jail and less than two weeks after I arrested him, Felder went up to a lady outside her house in Westlake Hills asking if he could mow her yard for $20. She refused, went into her house, locked the door, and he and a woman left in a green pickup truck. He drove only about a block down the street before stopping and breaking into a house.

The owners, Mr. and Mrs. Ivan Stout, happened to be out for a walk at the time. Mrs. Stout came home first and surprised the burglar and his companion in the act of ransacking their posh home. Felder had found Stout's guns and used one of them to beat the 69-year-old Mrs. Stout. When her husband returned a few minutes later, Felder turned on him and beat him to death.

The retired engineer's body lay on the driveway leading to his home. His wife was in the back yard, severely injured but still alive. A doctor living in the neighborhood treated Mrs. Stout at the scene before she was sent to the hospital. She was able to give police a partial license plate number and said she had been attacked by a man who had been driving a green pickup. Near Stout's body, we found a fragment that looked like it was from a wooden handle of a pistol. APD dispatchers told all officers to be on the lookout for a green pickup with the partial license plates we had.

All this had happened in the late afternoon. About 8 p.m. that day, the department received a call about a shooting at a residence in the 6100 block of Fairway in South Austin. On arrival, I saw parked outside the house a green pickup truck with a license plate matching the numbers we had. In the truck, we found a pistol with a piece of wood broken off from the grip. Later, a forensic examination showed that the fragment came from the pistol used in the Stout homicide.

Felder's estranged wife lived at the house on Fairway. Witnesses said he went to her door asking to come inside and she told him no. He then kicked the door in and Mrs. Beverly Felder hurried her children upstairs. Felder had left Stout's pistol in his truck, but Mrs. Felder had a shotgun and knew how to use it. As he backed her toward a bedroom, she pulled the trigger and dropped him in his tracks. He died where he fell. She was afraid of him and had good reason to be. As we began our investigation at the scene, an officer found Stout's wallet in Felder's pocket. It had been only three hours since he killed Stout and left Mrs. Stout for dead.

I thought that would be the end of this bizarre and tragic case until I learned that the Stout family had filed a $4 million lawsuit against the City of Austin and AAA Bonding Co. The plaintiffs claimed that the city was liable for the death of Stout as well as the injuries to Mrs. Stout. The premise of the lawsuit was that Felder, at the time he committed the crimes against the Stouts, was out on a $5,000 surety bond that should have been higher.

Though I had nothing to do with setting Felder's bond or the fact that it had been made by AAA Bonding, I was named as a defendant along with the city since I had been the last officer to arrest Felder. In Texas, judges are not subject to prosecution for actions they take while on the bench.

The case went to trial before a jury in early 1980. I can understand why the Stout family filed the suit. It was sad for all involved. I could not help but believe the judge who reduced the bond did not have all the information about Felder. The trial lasted two weeks. It was a difficult, unusual case having many complicated and emotional aspects. Attorneys for the city were Jim R. Weaver and Mary Ford. They did an outstanding job.

I was on the witness stand for several hours, most of my testimony concerning the arrest of Felder. I testified that I had been afraid of Felder, thought he was a danger to others and should not have been released from jail. I said that the other officers and I had risked our lives to arrest Felder. I looked directly at the jury and said, "We did our job--what else could your police department have possibly done?"

The jury returned a verdict favorable to the city and the bonding company, denying any recovery for the plaintiffs. The case did result in a determination that the city would be required to take some remedial action in the area of providing accurate and timely criminal record information to Municipal Court judges. Because of this case, city staff and the court made a lot of changes to improve communication with all involved. Felder should have never gotten out of jail.

This incident stands out in my memory because it left me a permanent reminder. To this day, I am still having trouble with my shoulder because of the injury I got when Felder threw me against the doorframe that night.

Traffic Stop Leads to Death of our Pet

Officers were working radar one day in the Wooten Elementary school zone in the 1400 block of West Anderson Lane. When I stopped by to see how they were doing, they were talking to a violator they had stopped. About the same time, the radar in my unit showed a vehicle approaching at 44 mph. The school zone was posted 20 mph, so I pulled the car over.

"What do you want?" the driver asked sarcastically as I walked up to his car.

"Your driver's license, please sir," I replied. He had his family in the car with him. He handed me his DL and I told him I was going to issue him a citation for speeding in a school zone. While I was writing the ticket, he told his young son to stick his tongue out at me. I tried to ignore that as I had him sign the ticket, and told him what he needed to do to handle it. He left mad, talking in Spanish.

About three weeks later, I was subpoenaed to Municipal Court on the citation. At that time, Judge Ronnie Earle was presiding judge. In the hearing, the man I had issued the ticket to said that he hadn't been speeding and knew the law. He really made a butt out of himself in court. Earle found him guilty and he paid a fine.

The next night I started getting hang-up phone calls. After three nights, it began to get old. I had a suspicion it was the man I had ticketed. I went back and checked the citation and saw that he lived in the 7800 block of Lazy Lane, just around the corner from where I lived.

I soon began to see his car parked across the street from my house. After dinner one evening, I put my gun on and started toward the car. When he saw me, he took off.

The nighttime calls kept up. I bought a tape recorder and recorded this message: "Mr. [I'll withhold his name], if this is you and you want to talk to me, I will be knocking on your door. Please talk to me if you are man enough." That night the phone rang about 1:00 a.m. I turned the recorder on, laid the phone by it, and took off for his house just around the corner. There were no lights on and no one answered the door, but the phone calls stopped.

We had a pretty little fox terrier that stayed in our fenced-in back yard. Our children truly loved the dog and so did I. One morning as I was going to work, I saw our dog laying in the back yard. When I went to him, he was dead. I took him to our veterinarian who called me later and said our family pet had been poisoned. He said it looked like someone had put rat poison (arsenic) on a piece of meat and fed it to our dog. It wasn't any mystery as to who had done it.

I had a talk with Chief Miles who wanted me to let the department handle it. Unfortunately, I didn't have much evidence, just suspicion. As it turned out, the man was in the U.S. on a visa from Argentina teaching a class at UT. When an investigator talked with his wife, she said that she had caught him in bed with their 16-year-old daughter. She also told him that her husband had it in for me and that he had poisoned our dog. Beyond that, she said her husband was planning to try to frame me by hiding some money at my house and reporting that I stole it.

The Chief was able to have his visa revoked and he got deported back to Argentina. I am glad it turned out that way. When he started hurting my family, he was very close to getting himself hurt.

Zeus Eats a Hamburger

When a Westlake Hills Police Department unit started chasing a stolen vehicle, our officers responded to assist when the car continued into Austin. As the vehicle headed north on Lamar Boulevard, it wrecked out at 29th Street and Lamar. When I drove up, Sgt. Greg Lasley was already at the scene. He told me that two people had run from the car. We caught one, but lost the other along Shoal Creek, west of Lamar. I called for our K9 unit, Officer David Koschel and his dog, Zeus.

Lasley and I didn't find any weapons or contraband in the car, but we did discover two half-eaten hamburgers. With Zeus on a leash, Koschel took him to the car. Zeus sniffed around and, before Koschel could stop him, gulped down one of the partial burgers. Koschel pulled him out of the car and Zeus started following the suspect's scent trail. But he made it only about 30 yards before he turned around and went back to the car and ate the other burger.

Koschel pulled him out of the car, scolded him and commanded, "Zeus, track! That's enough eating!" Zeus started tracking north along the creek. After about 400 yards, Zeus went across the creek bed to some tall grass on the west bank and began to act aggressively, as he was trained to do. Koschel turned him loose and he went into the grass and started to dig.

We couldn't figure out why he was doing that until we heard someone screaming and Koschel rushed in to get the dog off him. As it turned out, the suspect had dug a hole in the soft dirt and buried himself in the tall grass.

We turned the two men over to Westlake Hills Police Department, Chief David Gruetzmer. We would not have found the subject who ran had it not been for Koschel and his dog.

Zeus was a very special dog. He was later shot in the line of duty protecting Koschel.

Challenged to a Foot Race

We had a "close patrol" request to stop people from using a church parking lot in the 1700 block of East 12th Street. The church had a large parking lot and, on Sunday mornings when the taverns and dancehalls closed at 2 a.m., a steady stream of drivers pulled into the lot to continue their partying with plenty of drinking and fighting. When people showed up for church later in the morning, they would find the lot covered with trash, beer cans, bottles, and a few passed out drunks.

Ernie Hinkle

I was working the night shift and about 1 a.m. put two police units on the lot to prevent the crowd from gathering there. An hour later, we had a traffic jam because of all the cars driving around the area. The early morning hours are busy ones for police officers. The evening shift was supposed to get off at 3 a.m., but it was almost a given that they wouldn't get off until 5 or 6 a.m. I called Capt. Spohnholtz and asked him to have five of the officers ending their shift to meet me at 12th and Chicon to walk the area around the church until the crowd thinned out. We did this for four Saturday nights.

By the third Saturday night, we had made several buddies in the area and had some fun with them. One Sunday morning about 2 o'clock, five officers and I were standing on the corner of 12th and Chicon. I believe it was Sgt. Manuel Peña, Officer Todd Myers, Officer Norris (Spuds) McKenzie, Officer Wayne Simer, and Sgt. Greg Lasley. Several young men approached us and jokingly said that they could outrun us. One of them looked at me and said, "No way can you beat me in a foot race." He was drinking a little—just enough to make him think he was fast. "Let's get it on," I said. We closed the 1200 block of Chicon and ran several races. I raced the guy who had challenged me and had him beat from the start. About halfway down the block, I turned around to run backwards. To the delight of officers and spectators, I tripped and fell, busting my butt. But the kid was so slow I got up and still beat him. Todd and Spuds raced two other people and beat them both. I wasn't all that fast, but Todd and Spuds were.

Somehow, the chief found out about our race and wasn't real pleased with the way I handled the close patrol. But the church was glad their parking lot stayed free of drunks and the trash they would leave behind. After we had worked the area for about a month, it seemed to stop the problem and the closing-hour crowd found another place to congregate. I felt we also had demonstrated that we were people in the uniform—not just a uniform. However, that was the last time I closed a street down for a footrace.

Murder of an Outstanding Officer

My shift was working nights on May 18, 1978 when Officer Ralph Ablanedo was shot and killed. Ablanedo was a very dedicated officer, well liked by everyone who knew him. He always followed safety procedures. He wore a protective vest and made sure his fellow officers did, too.

Early that Thursday morning he had made a traffic stop in the 900 block of Live Oak Street near Travis High School in South Austin.

Then he stopped a red 1965 Mustang on Oltorf Street, just east of IH-35. The driver was a young woman later identified as Sheila Meinert. Sitting next to her in the front passenger seat was a man named David Lee Powell. After looking in the car and checking the occupants, Ralph radioed asking for a warrant check on both of them. He decided to let them go and they drove off. While he was getting back into his unit, the dispatcher advised that Powell had an outstanding warrant. Ralph replied that he had let the car go but would stop it again.

As Ralph was walking up to the vehicle, Powell shot him from inside the car through the back window with an AK-47 Russian-made submachine gun. The bullets ripped through Ralph's protective vest, hitting him ten times in the chest. We could all hear Ralph screaming on the radio. His close friend, Bruce Mills, was the first officer to reach the scene. As other officers arrived, a gunfight broke out on Oltorf Street just around the corner from the 900 block of Live Oak. Powell threw a hand grenade toward the officers who were coming after him. Thank God, it didn't go off.

Sheila Meinert had a .45 semi-automatic pistol and tried to shoot another officer, but she was taken into custody without anyone getting hurt, including her. Powell escaped after an exchange of gunfire and ran into a large field just behind and south of (what was then) Travis High School. I was at the scene, but I badly wanted to go to the hospital to be with Ralph. Before I could get away, I received a call that Ralph had died. Now what I wanted to do was get Powell, one way or another. I called most of our platoon out to our location leaving only one officer for each sector.

We set up a perimeter around the field where Powell was likely hiding. We were approximately 20 feet apart and had units patrolling the outer area. I was worried that he might try to get into the school, so I put two officers on top of it. My plan was that as soon as we had daylight, we would start walking through the field.

We started at dawn. All the officers were more than ready. They had wanted to go into the field immediately, but I knew that was too dangerous and held them back. Just after we started, Powell was spotted under some bushes on the west side of the school and arrested. We were very lucky to get him before anyone else got hurt.

Now my thoughts turned to Ralph's family. Usually, the last things I would say to our platoon before we hit the streets was, "Be careful! One of the most important things you have to do tonight is go home in the morning." Ralph did not have a chance. His beautiful wife, Judith, and two young sons were left without a husband and father due to a no-good drug head.

Officers found a duffle bag of methamphetamines hanging in a tree not far from where we captured Powell. His fingerprints were on the bag. In the follow-up investigation, we learned that he was running a speed factory out of his house in the 700 block of Water Street. The speed-producing equipment and supplies, another hand grenade, and explosive recipes were confiscated from his residence.

Later, detectives learned that Powell was a brilliant physics student at UT who had dropped out of school in 1976 a few hours shy of a degree.

The loss of Ralph and the impact it had on his family at home and to our family at work left a big hole in our hearts. Knowing our job must go on, we turned toward supporting Ralph's family in any way we could.

I was asked to do Ralph's eulogy. I was honored, but scared to death. I just didn't think I was capable of doing as good a job as I wanted to do. But I agreed to do it, wanting to do it for Ralph, his family, and our department. I went to talk with Monsignor Fred Bomar and he helped me a lot. I also talked to Rev. Roger Wilson who conducted the services for Ralph.

The services were held at 10 a.m. the following Saturday at Hyltin Manor Funeral Home, 3000 N. IH-35. Graveside services were at Fiskville Cemetery in far North Austin.

I prayed that I could do a good job with the eulogy. I spent two days and nights preparing for it, one of the hardest things I had ever done. Without God being with me, I could never have done it. When I began, my voice wavered and I was perilously close to tears, but I was able to get hold of my feelings. This was Ralph's tribute:

"We are here this morning to express our respect, affection and our gratitude for Ralph Ablanedo and to pay tribute to a police officer, a husband, a father, a son, and to us, a dear friend.

Ralph Ablanedo was born April 27, 1952 in Frankfurt, Germany. His parents are Mr. and Mrs. Armand Ablanedo. Ralph moved to Austin with his parents in 1965. He graduated from Reagan High School and attended St. Edward's University. He is survived by his loving wife, Judith, and their two sons, Steve and David, and by his two sisters, Irene and Arlene, and his brother, Armand.

Ralph Ablanedo was employed by the Austin Police Department on Jan. 4, 1972 as a police aide. He was commissioned as a police officer on April 27, 1973. He was a member of The First Church of the Nazarene and a member of Onion Creek Masonic Lodge.

Most of you know these facts ... because you are all the loving family of Ralph Ablanedo-- you, his wife, his parents, his brother and sisters, and his close friends are the family Ralph loved so much! You are the ones for whom he loved and lived and worked! You understood him best, and so you loved him the most! It is right and proper then that we are the ones who gather to pay him tribute and respect. Ralph would want his family and his friends around him.

Crime is an ugly occurrence in modern society. It has always been and now continues in epidemic proportion. It takes unbroken belief and courage and persistence to hit the streets every day and night as a police officer...to keep faith in the system, to guarantee justice to social and moral degenerates you know are guilty, to lay life and limb on the line and then to know whatever you do, you are liable to get as much or more criticism than applause!

Our society asks a great deal of its police officers. We expect that they will not only enforce the law, but also wear the hat of the curbside psychiatrist, the social worker, legal adviser, minister, and sometimes, the doctor.

Few officials in our society are given the breadth of discretion and heavy responsibility that our police are asked to carry on -- matters affecting the lives of millions of Americans. Law officers on the firing line often have only minutes—or even seconds (and in Ralph's case, not even seconds)—to make decisions on their conduct.

The patrol officer is literally the shield and buckle of our society. We expect of him honesty, courtesy, ability, intelligence, discipline, training, and understanding. Ralph passed all of these.

All of these virtues are required at all times of police officers, plus the ability to act quickly and, often, with inadequate information, but always with wisdom and discretion. And yet, a police officer is like any other person. He has the same hopes and joys, the same fears and frustrations, the same ambitions and dreams as any other person because he is also an ordinary man. Yet he has an extraordinary vocation—a most noble calling and, also, a very humbling one.

Ralph Ablanedo was a young man who possessed all these very noble qualities of his profession! He personified the dedicated public servant who put his life on the line so many times in ordinary and extraordinary ways. To his many friends and associates, Ralph's special sense of humor, along with his keen sense of responsibility, was an example of the code of the Austin Police Department. We will deeply miss him.

On behalf of the Austin Police Department, we extend our very deepest sympathy to you, the members of Ralph's family.

Lt. Ernest Hinkle, Jr., #317"

David Powell was tried and sentenced to death within months of the shooting. His attorney appealed his conviction saying that he had talked to a psychiatrist without having been warned of his rights. As a result, he received a new trial in 1991. He was again found guilty and given the death penalty. Once more, Powell appealed that guilty verdict on the basis that he had been improperly sentenced. Given a new sentencing trial in 1999, he was, for the third time, given the death penalty.

His lawyers appealed that decision to the 5th Circuit Court of Appeals and lost.

The Ablanedo family had to go through 30 years of appeals. That is a bunch of crap. The execution was finally carried out in mid-2010. Before the execution, Powell wrote a letter to the family admitting his guilt and apologizing for what he did. Apologies do not bring back a husband, father, and friend.

Bank Robbery

In the early 1970s, there was a Bank of America on the northeast corner of Congress Avenue and 5th Street. Also, the Greyhound Bus Station was in the 400 block of Congress on the east side of the street.

I was just leaving the police station around 11 a.m. when the dispatcher put out a "robbery in progress" call at the bank. I got there almost immediately meeting a bank vice president at the lobby door. He told me that the subject had just left running south down the alley off 5th Street. He described the robber as being a white male about six feet tall wearing a brown ski mask, a green shirt and blue jeans, armed with a pistol.

Having worked a walking beat in that area, I was well familiar with it. I drove the length of the alley all the way to 2nd Street and then doubled back to 4th Street where the bus station was. I felt that would be a logical stop for him. I checked a dumpster in the alley behind the bus station and found a green button-up shirt and the ski mask.

I went in the back door of the station and talked with the ticket agent. He said no buses had left the depot, but one would be leaving in about 15 minutes. Looking around the depot, I saw a white male wearing a white T-shirt sitting in the back corner. I asked the agent about him and he said he couldn't remember seeing him in the station before then. I started walking like I was headed out the front door, then hustled to his seat and arrested him. He didn't have a gun, but his pockets were full of money. I took him back to the bank and he was positively identified as the robber. By now, FBI agents were at the bank and took charge of the subject and the investigation.

The "D" Word

In 1978, my wife Jean and I divorced after 25 years of marriage. As our children grew up, Jean and I had grown apart. We parted as friends, still are, and always will be. Jean helped me study for promotional exams and was always supportive.

Police work is hard on family life. I was mostly working nights and weekends. For vacation, we would go back to my home in Kentucky every year. I always tried to make it a fun trip, going different directions each time, going by the zoo in Memphis, to Mammoth Cave, or to Rock City in Tennessee. Even at that, I am sure it got boring going to Kentucky every year. The family always supported me, but I am sure the hours I kept, always working weekends and hardly ever getting home on time, were all factors in our divorce.

Our two children, Ricky Allan Hinkle and Vickie Hinkle (now Vickie Baker), were a joy and the best part of my life. The divorce bothered them, but they wanted both of us to be happy. They grew up to be very responsible, hard-working, and fun-loving parents. Ricky retired from the department in 2009 with the rank of commander, roughly the equivalent of a captain in my time. Vickie and her husband, Greg Baker, have their own business, Hollis Baker Sign Shop in Austin. They are truly a joy in our family.

We enjoy a close-knit family and it is special when we can all be together. The grandchildren are so very wonderful and make life great. I am truly blessed.

Aqua Fest Boat Races

On July 10-11, 1978, one of the Aqua Fest events was boat racing on Town Lake, just east of IH-35. The spectators would gather along the north side of the lake at Festival Beach.

Ernie Hinkle

A group known as the Brown Berets was protesting the boat races and doing anything it could to stop or interfere with them. There were not that many Brown Berets, maybe 20 to 30, but they were experienced agitators. They would get rabble-rousers from UT as well as some out-of-town help.

The mayor and our department had meetings with the protestors in an attempt to satisfy their objections, but it was hard to tell what they really wanted. They said they were supporting East Austin neighborhoods, but a survey showed that East Austin people, by a huge majority, had no objection to the races. On top of that, most of the protesting Brown Berets didn't even reside in East Austin.

The only purpose I could see for them to protest the boat races was to build a decisive power base for a small handful of agitators and, in doing this, they seemed to be quite successful. They got the city council to allow only one entrance to the beach area. That, I knew, was going to be a problem for the police. To get to the area, vehicles would have to take the turnaround under IH-35 and enter Festival Beach from the East Frontage Road—all one-way roadways.

Around 9 a.m. on the first day of the races, a large crowd and a good number of participants began arriving. The protestors tried to get the race fans involved; but, for the most part, the spectators ignored the Brown Berets despite their back-alley language.

Assigned to work the boat races were Capt. Gilbert Miller, Capt. John Vasquez, and my platoon. My platoon worked great as a team, and did we ever have our hands full. One of the protestors swam out to where the starting lights were for the boats and was trying to break them. He was arrested without incident. Next, the Brown Berets started standing in front of cars coming into the beach area. We arrested them for the misdemeanor offense of being "pedestrians in the roadway." Then they staged a collision between two cars to block the only access for spectators, but we pushed them out of the way. Next a rear window was broken out of a vehicle coming into the beach. A witness saw the protestor who broke the window and he got arrested. After that, they drove six older vehicles to the turnaround under the interstate and locked the doors, completely blocking the roadway to the races. The drivers ran off and we had wreckers haul the cars to the Police Pound only holding up traffic for a few minutes.

As I remember, we made about 18 arrests on both days of the races. The event went off without a big problem despite the best efforts of the Brown Berets. The beach was crowded with spectators both days.

Lt. Ernie Hinkle and Officer Vernon Crumley working the Austin Aqua Fest Boat Races on Town Lake -August 1978.

Working Prostitution on South Congress Avenue

In the early 1980s, prostitution was almost out of hand on South Congress Avenue from around the 600 block south to Oltorf Street. As time permitted, district officers would work that area as often as possible when not on calls. Sr. Sgt. Gene Freudenberg, sector sergeant of David Sector in South Austin, worked that area hard. It was decided to put one officer on special assignment in street clothes in their personal car to work that area. Gene put Officer Bruce Lutringer on this assignment. Bruce owned a beautiful Mustang and had a six-pack of beer in the car that was probably a four-pack after he drank a couple. At any rate, it worked. Bruce made several cases that night. That procedure worked quite well. Prostitution began to go undercover and was not so much out in the open.

Sgt. Freudenberg was very successful at cleaning up the prostitution on South Congress Avenue, arresting some of the johns, as well. He is now retired.

Officer Bruce Lutringer later became sergeant over the motorcycles being highly respected as a supervisor by his officers. He retired in 2012.

Bruce was telling me his wife rode with him one time when he was working radar on IH-35. He was chasing vehicles most of the night. As you can imagine, for a rider, this can be a harrowing experience, especially if one is not use to it. After they got home in the early morning, his wife told him she didn't think it was worth risking both of their lives the way he was driving and that she was never going to ride with him again—and she didn't.

KKK Marches and Demonstrations

In February 1983, the department received information that the Ku Klux Klan planned to come to Austin for a protest. They applied for a permit and requested police protection. That generated quite a bit of publicity. As I remember, their permit was for March 19, 1983. The department began to make plans to protect them and then get them out of town.

The Klan agreed to a staging area at the northwest corner of 14th and Trinity Streets. They also agreed to keep their guns locked in the trunks of their cars and to allow themselves to be searched before starting on the march. The approved route was for them to walk in their white robes west on 11th to the Capitol, go around the Capitol to 13th Street, then east on 13th Street back to the staging area.

Our platoon, headed by Capt. Gerald Spohnholtz and Capt. Ray Sanders, began to train for the march. We were told there could be anywhere from 100 to 1,000 Klansmen showing up for the march. A command center was set up at headquarters only seven blocks from the staging area: Lt. Alvin DeVane was in charge of communications, which would be on a separate radio channel; Lt. Olan Kelley was to have bomb dogs available to check suspicious cars; Det. Capt. Pete Neal along with Det. Sgts. James Baker and Jimmy Hemphill would be positioned along the route to keep an eye out for trouble.

We would have photographers with Polaroid cameras at the paddy wagon to make photos of all arrested persons. Also, if we had time, the arresting officer would write a field arrest offense report. My platoon was going to be responsible for the staging area and areas along 11th Street. We felt we were well prepared to handle the march.

About two days before the demonstration, we began to get information that the Brown Berets would be there starting trouble. We had photos of several Brown Berets to be on the lookout for.

We were also warned that the John Brown Anti-Klan Organization planned to be there. We were also advised to be on the lookout for a late-model Chevrolet pickup, silver/maroon, driven by a six-foot male with bushy, reddish hair who had an extreme hatred for blacks and policemen. This person had fired several shots at a cross burning in Houston where four such cross burnings had taken place in the past two weeks. We had additional information that a motorcycle gang from Oklahoma called the "Nomads" had taken interest in the march. The report was that they had purchased 9mm pistols and body armor in Houston and, if they came, they would not fly their colors. We were further advised that a subject identified as Michael Douglas Lowe, also known as "Mad Bomber," might take this opportunity to use violence and that he had an extreme hatred for police. He had been a Klan member, but got booted for advocating extreme violence. He was reported to be living in Waco.

We were getting a lot of information with very little time to do much with it other than to alert all of our officers.

The demonstration was to start at 1 p.m. on March 19th. About 11 a.m., officers arrested a subject in the 1000 block of Guadalupe carrying a rifle and shotgun. He had a flyer about the Klan march. All officers were at their assigned locations by noon. Sometimes our best planning went to hell in a hand basket, which is what happened this time.

[147]

As the Klan began arriving at the staging area, a large crowd gathered around them. Capt. Sanders requested two squads from our platoon to meet him at the staging area. At that point, our prearranged plans were put aside. I took Sgt. Charles Hickey's and Sgt. Elbert Frank's squads, a total of 18 officers, to the staging area. It was decided that this group would walk with the Klan. We started the march going west on 11th from Trinity Street.

Despite all the big numbers we had been hearing, only 18 Klan members had shown up for the march. However, there were 300 to 400 anti-Klan protestors and some were harassing the Klan members. As we were walking down the street on the route, the spectators started following the Klan. We had officers in front, on both flanks, and in the back. It seemed to be going well but, the farther we walked, the larger the crowd got around the Klan.

When we got to the Capitol and started moving north up the sidewalk to the front of the building, we were able to divert a lot of the spectators from the group. The Capitol was locked and DPS troopers stood at each door. As we were walking on the sidewalk on the east side of the Capitol, I was flanking the Grand Wizard. That's when some spectators started throwing eggs and tomatoes. I saw the Grand Wizard get hit in the head with a paper bag of feces. He asked us what we were going to do about it. I told him he could file a complaint if we could identify who threw it, but said my main priority was getting them out of there safely.

By then, we were behind the Capitol on Congress at 13th Street which is where a lot of the crowd had gathered. From there, we went east on 14th Street back to the staging area at Trinity. Along the way, we were all hit with rocks and eggs. Just before we reached the staging area, the Brown Berets tried breaking through the police line. Fists and batons were flying on both sides. I arrested the guy who seemed to be the leader of the Brown Berets and got him off to jail.

Back at the staging area, the Klan members started trying to get their guns out of the trunks of their cars. When an officer racked a shell in his shotgun and told them to leave their trunks closed, that got their attention. They got in their vehicles and motorcycle officers escorted them out of town.

The day after, we were criticized for the way the march was handled. The Brown Berets accused us of beating them and infringing on their Constitutional rights. Chief Frank Dyson, who had replaced Chief Miles following his retirement, called all supervisors who had been working the march to meet with him. He was upset with what he was hearing and with what some of the news media were reporting. I told the chief the only people who had been abused were the police and that I thought that our officers had done a good job and I was proud of them. That was the consensus of all supervisors before we left the meeting. By TV news time that evening, after his investigation and having viewed the film footage of the march, the chief said in interviews that some members of the Brown Beret were nothing but hoodlums and that his officers had done a good job. No one got hurt, and we made only two arrests. Dyson had nothing but praise for the way his officers handled the situation, which easily could have turned deadly.

1987 KKK March - Lt. Ernie Hinkle trying to direct protestors to get out of the street.

Ernie Hinkle

Shooting Incident Involving a Police Officer

Around 12:30 a.m. on Oct. 13, 1984, Sr. Sgt. Elbert Franks responded to a disturbance call in the 2000 block of East 2nd Street. The dispatcher had advised him that there were subjects in the street hollering and blocking traffic. On arrival, he saw two people in the street–one of them was trying to get the other one out of the street.

The subject I will refer to as Mark refused to get out of the street. As the sergeant approached him, he saw that Mark had a knife with what looked like about a four-inch blade on his belt. When Franks asked him to please get out of the street, he told the sergeant he was a "time traveler" and he didn't have to.

At that point, the sergeant moved toward Mark to disarm him. But Mark moved away and pulled the knife. The sergeant attempted to talk Mark into dropping the knife and, at one point, he did so. When Franks tried to get Mark to back away from the knife, the man picked up the knife, lunged forward, and stabbed Franks in the chest.

Mark then ran in a southwesterly direction. Mark stopped, turned toward Franks again with the knife, and the sergeant fired two shots. This time Mark fell to the ground.

Dr. Robert Bayardo, Chief Medical Examiner, performed the autopsy on Mark. The postmortem showed he had been shot twice—a grazing wound to his right shoulder and a second, fatal wound, to the face. Bayardo ruled the death a justifiable homicide.

The shooting was reviewed by executive staff and it was their decision that the shooting was justifiable. The case was "no-billed" by the Travis County Grand Jury.

That incident is just one example of the kind of situation that no officer wants to be involved in. However, there are times when an officer has no choice when it comes to protecting himself or a fellow citizen.

Honor Guard

The APD Honor Guard is made up of handpicked officers who are dedicated to honoring fallen officers and otherwise representing the department in a professional way. Credit for this unit mostly goes to Commander Jim O'Leary and Lt. Tim Krista. O'Leary took pride in this unit, worked diligently in recruiting first-rate officers and training with them on a regular basis.

In 1985, I sent O'Leary a memo requesting to be a member of the Honor Guard. Sometime later, he came by my office and tried to diplomatically tell me he didn't think he had a spot in the unit for me. Actually, when I sent the memo, I was just jacking with him. I was 53 years old. All the other officers in the unit were much younger and in excellent physical condition.

When O'Leary turned me down, I said, "Okay, Jim. I will start to practice for the unit and try again." After that, whenever I saw O'Leary in his office, I would march up and down the hall outside calling cadence, stopping to salute him, and performing a parade rest. Sometimes he would just close the door to his office.

Commander O'Leary and Lt. Krista are fine officers very much respected by their colleagues. Anything they did was top-notch, particularly the APD Honor Guard.

After I had been retired for a number of years, at a luncheon on February 19, 2009, the commander presented me with an Honorary Commission as a member of APD Honor Guard.

Ernie Hinkle

Assigned to City Council Chambers

On June 7, 1990, the city council was holding a hearing on the Barton Creek Zoning Ordinance. More than 800 people had signed up to speak. Some of those speakers were considered potentially violent.

With around 1,800 people on hand, I was called to the council chambers on West 2nd Street to handle crowd control. The chambers were too small for all of the people to get in and they had spilled out into the street. I took six officers, putting two outside and one standing on each side of the council members, mainly for a show of force. The Fire Department was monitoring the number of people allowed inside.

I walked both inside and outside talking to as many people as possible and asked the officers to do the same. It was essential not to let the situation get out of control. All the officers were courteous and informative when dealing with the public and city staff. On two occasions, a speaker got loud and was asked by the mayor to leave because his allotted time at the podium was up. I escorted them out of the chambers, told them to please calm down, and they both left.

We overlooked some minor offenses to keep from making a bigger problem. The officers did a great job in maintaining a very orderly tone for the entire 17 hours we were there. It was a very long day and we were walking on eggshells, but we succeeded in keeping the peace.

Citizen Asked for Directions to East 6th Street

Capt. Spohnholtz didn't like to stay behind a desk. He enjoyed working the streets, and often rode with me. He was a great person, very dedicated to law enforcement and well-liked by the 70 officers in his platoon. We had a lot of good times together and did a lot of police work, including making back-up calls in addition to being supervisors. Being on the streets with the troops made for good morale, and we enjoyed doing it.

One Friday about 12:30 a.m., we were on Ben White Boulevard near the Congress Avenue exit when we saw a young woman running in the roadway. I drove up beside her, but that didn't seem to faze her—she just kept running.

I got behind her and said to the captain, "Since I'm driving, I'll pull up in front of her and you can jump out and grab her." That plan worked well only until the captain took hold of her arm. Then the crap hit the fan. She started fighting and it took both of us to control her. She was a small woman and the captain and I were big men, but she was fighting drunk and darn good at it. We finally got her cuffed and in the police unit. I put her in the right front passenger seat and the captain got in the back seat. She was very violent, screaming, and trying to kick out my front window.

As we started to jail with her going north on Congress, she managed to get out of one of her handcuffs and started hitting me with the other cuff. Turned out her wrists were so small that she could just slip her hands out of them. She was knocking the crap out of me with the one cuff so the captain reached over and pulled her in the back seat with him.

Again, the fight was on. He finally got her under moderate control by sitting on her. At that point, I slowed down to watch the fight. She wasn't happy and she was very vulgar.

I had stopped for a red light at Congress and Oltorf when a car pulled up next to me and the driver asked for directions to East 6th Street. As I was directing him, the female the captain was sitting on started screaming, "Rape, rape." The car drove off and the captain said, "Hinkle, go Code 3 and get me to the jail—don't stop and give anyone else directions!"

When we got to the jail, we had to put her in a straitjacket to keep her from hurting herself. I later found out she was on LSD. After she was booked, the captain looked like he had been hit with a Mac truck. "Hinkle, I am going back to my office," is all he said.

The troops found out about it and kidded us about a little woman kicking our butts. They suggested that we might want to start working out, running and all that kind of stuff. I can only imagine what the people in the car asking directions thought when she started screaming, "Rape."

Solving a Little Matter of Jealousy

Another night when the captain was riding with me, we came up on a couple having a big argument. I stopped to break it up. They were drinking, but not drunk enough to arrest.

It seemed as though the girl had been dancing with another man when her date got jealous and pulled her out of El Toro Bar. I put the female in my car and went over to where the captain was talking with her boyfriend.

The captain was really building him up. He told him he was too handsome to be fighting over a woman and that, with his good looks, he could get any number of dates he wanted. Soon the guy was agreeing with him and admitted that he was too good looking to be worried about someone taking his woman. After listening to that conversation, I went back and told the female she was too pretty to let someone like her boyfriend push her around. She told me she thought so, too, and wasn't going to let anyone push her around anymore.

The guy went back into the club and the captain and I dropped the female off at her residence. Hopefully, their new sense of self-esteem kept them out of fights after that. At least, I never handled them again.

On Holy Ground

It seemed we were always having winos congregating and sleeping on the front porch of the Catholic Church in the 2000 block of Guadalupe. We would drive by there and, before running them off, make them clean up all their empty bottles and other trash. One night when Capt. Spohnholtz was riding with me, I saw a wino peeing beside the church.

"Look! That guy is peeing on the holy ground," I told the captain who I knew was a devout Catholic. I stopped and Spohnholtz bailed out to take off after him. They ran down an alley behind the church and I lost sight of them. As I was driving around looking for them, I found the captain on San Antonio Street about five blocks from the church. He had lost sight of the subject, and there were plenty of places to hide in that area.

I kidded the captain about being outrun by a drunk. He said that I couldn't have done any better, and that the guy had just hidden somewhere. I had recognized the church desecrator and kept driving around in the area looking for him.

When I drove past a car wash on 19th Street, there he was, taking a bath in the car wash. This wasn't unusual for winos to do; and in this case, it gave the captain a reason to arrest him for being nude in a public place.

The next day when we went to work, he was still in jail. Spohnholtz went up and made a deal with him—if he would agree to help the church area stay clean and not leave trash all around the main entrance, he would drop the charges against him. He agreed to that, and when he was let out of jail, I saw the captain slip him some money.

For some time afterward, whenever we drove by the church the guy would be there keeping things under control. You would think he had been commissioned as a police officer. He even had some of his buddies helping him keep the trash picked up.

I stopped by the church early one night and asked him if he would help me pull a joke on the captain. He said he would be happy to. When I went to pick up the captain, I took the wino with me. I called the captain and said I was waiting for him on the west lot at headquarters. It was a dark area. I gave the wino my police cap and had him get in the driver's seat. Meanwhile, I took off and hid. When the captain came out, you could have heard him a block away yelling, "What are you doing driving a police car and where in the hell is Hinkle?"

Bull's Eye?

Capt. Spohnholtz was an expert marksman. He taught at the pistol range where we had to qualify monthly. I was never a great shot, but had no trouble qualifying.

The captain and I would usually go to the range together. One day, just as we started shooting, I discretely aimed at his target instead of mine, aiming for the white area. When he saw a hit out of the bull's eye on his target, he started looking at his gun. On my next shot, I aimed at his target again, punching another hole in the white. He again saw a hit out of the bull's eye and called for the range officer to come check his weapon.

When he realized nothing was wrong with his pistol, the captain walked down to his target and saw he had two hits in the bull's eye. He also saw there were four hits on his target and that my target was clean. I had to wait until he qualified before I could shoot again.

The Survey

One of my fellow lieutenants was Fred Williams. He was extremely upset because Burleson Road, the street he lived on, was going to be widened taking up some of his front yard. We listened to Fred complain about this for over a month. He was almost obsessed about losing part of his yard.

Capt. Spohnholtz and I decided we would really give him something to complain about. I had a friend in the surveying business and got him to get me some survey markers. Early one quiet, cold morning around 3 a.m., we went to Burleson Road and put the survey markers about five feet from Fred's house. To make it look official, we decided to put a few more out along the block. That part of the joke wasn't a good plan.

At work the next night, the lieutenant was hot. "After the survey," he said, "I will have less than five feet to the roadway and that is in violation of city restrictions." Turns out, he had called the city building inspection office and they had agreed to meet with residents living in that block of Burleson Road. The lieutenant didn't ask if we knew anything about it and I sure didn't volunteer any information.

A few days later, Fred told us that the survey crew had made a mistake and that he was only losing three to five feet of his yard. He did say that the ordeal had brought all of his neighbors together to better support the area where they lived.

Fred suspected I was involved in putting out the bogus survey markers, but he wasn't sure. He did know we were working the night they appeared. A year after Fred retired I sent him a Christmas card and signed it, "The Surveyor."

Traffic Stop Shootings

Anyone who has been in law enforcement very long knows there is no such thing as a routine traffic stop. The same can be said about family disturbance calls. You just never know what the next call or traffic stop will bring.

[157]

We were working the night shift on November 26, 1991 when at 12:25 a.m. we began to get reports of shootings in the 900 to 1100 blocks of East 12th Street. In the 900 block, we found someone shot in the mouth. I was at that location getting a description of the gunman, a middle-aged male who had threatened to shoot everyone he encountered, when I heard a unit go out on a traffic stop in the 1100 block.

Officers Don Mayes, Gerardo "Jerry" Gonzalez and other officers were out of their patrol cars and several people were standing on the sidewalk watching them. That's when a man in the crowd told the bystanders that he was going to shoot the officers. Fortunately, someone told Officer Mayes.

Armed with a shotgun, a pistol, and a knife, the man who had made the threat began walking toward the officers. The officers repeatedly told the man to stop. As he started to raise the shotgun, Mayes opened fire. The gunman died at the scene. The dead man fit the description of the person involved in the other three shootings we had in the same area. Officer Mayes' actions likely saved all the officers' lives. Now retired, he was a very good and well-liked officer.

The year before, we nearly lost another officer. On April 25, 1990, our platoon was working the night shift. About 2 a.m., Officer Gonzalez saw two men at the northeast corner of East 12th and Chicon Streets engaged in what appeared to be a narcotics transaction. Gonzalez pretended not to see the subjects and acted as if he was leaving the area. After he was out of their sight, Gonzalez turned his vehicle around and headed back to 12th and Chicon. When the pair saw him, they started walking away from the area together. Gonzalez pulled into a driveway in front of them and quickly exited his vehicle telling them he wanted to talk to them.

At that time in the morning, traffic is usually very heavy on the police radio. Consequently, Gonzalez was unable to advise the dispatcher prior to attempting to detain the subjects. He asked the men to place their hands on the police unit where he could see them. One subject, later identified as Johnny Byrd, stopped in front of Gonzalez's police unit while the other subject, later identified as Gerald Clarke, stopped by the left front of the police unit.

Gonzalez told Byrd several times that he needed to come around to the front of his vehicle while showing his hands. Byrd did not come around the vehicle but made furtive movements toward his back while at the same time saying that he did not have anything on him. Clarke, however, was compliant and put his hands on the police unit. Meanwhile, Byrd continued to act nervous.

Moments later, Byrd came running around the car toward Gonzalez. The officer started backpedaling to create some distance between them when Byrd grabbed Gonzalez's shirt with his right hand. In his left hand, he held a .38 caliber derringer that had been hidden behind his back. Byrd pointed that small but deadly weapon at Officer Gonzalez's face at point-blank range and pulled the trigger.

Incredibly, the would-be cop killer missed. The bullet went between Officer Gonzalez's right ear and right arm, which he had instinctively raised in a defensive position. The officer suffered gunpowder burns to the inside of his right arm and a loud ringing in his right ear from the weapon being discharged. But, fortunately, he was not hit.

Officer Gonzalez struck Byrd across the head with his flashlight, knocking him to the ground and causing him to drop the small pistol. At about this time the officer heard a gunshot coming from the direction where Clarke was standing. Gonzalez looked up to see Clarke pointing a revolver at him. The other suspect had also shot at the officer and missed. Then he fired two more shots, also missing.

Taking cover behind his police unit, Officer Gonzalez shot at Clarke twice. By then, both subjects were running toward the north alley of East 12th Street. The officer chased them on foot, but lost them when they split up. Using his handheld radio, Gonzalez broadcasted information on the incident and described the suspects.

Clarke and Byrd were later apprehended and charged with attempted capital murder.

Ernie Hinkle

There is no question in my mind that God was riding with Officer Gonzalez that night. Sr. Sgt. Manuel Peña, his supervisor at that time, told me more than once what a special officer Gonzalez was. And, I was always impressed with him. He had a great attitude and just made you feel good when you were around him.

On January 29, 2014, Chief Art Acevedo awarded now Lt. Gerardo Gonzalez the Medal of Honor for his courageous actions in the foregoing incident. The award came 24 years after the fact, but very much deserved.

The Full Moon

That same night, just about as soon as I left the scene of the officer-involved shooting, I responded to a call on Allyson Court near Pleasant Valley Road and Stassney Lane where a 14-year-old had shot his 36-year-old father three times in the back.

As we put it together, the teenager had wanted to go out and his dad said no. We arrested the boy and took him to the Gardner House Juvenile Detention Facility.

Looking back, I have often wondered if there was a full moon that night. Turns out, it was a new moon, but we had shootings all over town. I am convinced there is something about a full moon that brings out the worst in people.

When I first started in law enforcement, my old sergeant told me, "We are going to be busy because the moon is full." I just laughed it off; but, over the years, I have come to believe it. I don't know what it is—maybe you can just see better at night when the moon is full.

CB Radios

During the early 1970s, citizens band radios were very popular. Sgt. Charlie Hickey, whose area covered IH-35, bought a CB and had it installed in his police unit. At night, IH-

35 was full of 18-wheelers coming through Austin and he started communicating with their drivers.

Charlie got to know their "handles" (call names) and would advise them of traffic problems. As long as they kept their speed down, they didn't have to worry about the cops in Austin. The truck drivers appreciated this and thought the sergeant walked on water.

On more than one occasion when we had a pursuit on IH-35, Charlie would contact an 18-wheeler and they would slow down, team up, and block the roadway. Austin cops were really popular with truckers passing through Austin, all because of Charlie. He didn't give them permission to do anything against the law, but let them know we were out there working just like they were. Our concern was to get them through Austin safely. I could never afford a CB radio, but I sure appreciated what the sergeant was doing with his.

About 1 o'clock one morning Capt. Spohnholtz and I were going east in the 800 block of 11th Street and drove up on a 1976 black Buick Roadmaster. It was a good-looking car. What attracted my attention to the car was it had radio antennas all over the trunk plus two whiplash antennas, one on each side of the car. Telling the captain that I just wanted to see this communication system, I pulled the car over.

"Sir," I said as we approached the driver, "you have done nothing wrong. You are driving well. I just wanted to see if you would let us see your communication system. I never saw so many antennas."

Slumping down in his seat, he said, "I haven't gotten around to putting radios in my car. I just like antennas."

I had a hard time keeping a straight face while telling him his antennas looked really good, radios or not.

Special Community Relations Task Force

In October 1974, the city council appointed a tri-ethnic task force of 17 citizens to study and evaluate the relationship between the community and the police department. The task force was further charged with reporting its findings and making recommendations to the council on ways to improve police community relations.

I was appointed to this task force which turned out to be a trying and difficult job. After our second meeting, it became obvious to me that a number of the committee members were headhunting. They wanted Chief Miles out.

The task force worked for nine months. It was too large of a group and, unfortunately, we spent most of our time arguing about a specific incident rather than focusing on improving relations or enhancing the department's image. It was hard for me to understand just what we were doing. It seemed more like an investigative body or a police review board. In the end, a number of the members dealt themselves out for various reasons leaving only a few active participants.

Because the task force was plagued by lack of a quorum in the last few weeks, Rev. Father Fred Bomar and I decided to write our own report to the council and turned it in on August 1, 1975 with the following recommendations:

1. Create a public school course taught by the Austin Police Department on the function of police officers and citizen rights.
2. Create a position for a professional counselor for police officers involved in serious accidents.
3. Create a police advisory board for citizen complaints.
4. Increase use of non-traffic citations in lieu of arresting people.
5. Upgrade police benefits and pay.
6. Increase minority recruiting.
7. Create provisions for psychological testing for officers.
8. Provide refresher courses for police officers.
9. Establish a citizen ride-along program.

10. Establish a practice that, when possible, officers would get out of their cars to meet the citizens rather than just when called.

This was the minority report that went to the council signed by Rev. Father Fred Bomar, Mrs. Amon Wroe, Mrs. Suyou Kemp, and me. The second report was presented by Dr. John Warfield.

Overall, the board had not been able to work together. I appreciated having the opportunity to represent the department, but I found it difficult at times to hear the many accusations against police officers and the department as a whole. All the people on the task force had their agendas. I did get to work with some great people and appreciated the many hours they devoted to improving the image of law enforcement.

Police Work to Make Old Shack into a Home

Sgt. Doyne Bailey knew an elderly lady, Ms. Hettie Jackson, living in only one room of an old house in the 1900 block of Rosewood Avenue. The house had no plumbing, no electricity, and cats and dogs ran in and out of half the rooms in the back. To enter it, you had to walk on the supporting boards of the floor to prevent falling through gaping holes to the ground below. The one room she was living in had no protection from the weather.

Ms. Jackson had lived in the house for 44 years and did not want to leave her home. She received a small Social Security check and had a hot meal every day from Meals on Wheels; but, mostly, she lived on sardines and cookies. She had a son in Philadelphia, but hadn't heard from him in years. Ms. Jackson seemed to have many friends in the area and would visit neighbors and take daily walks.

Sgt. Doyne Bailey took it upon himself to see that the house was made livable. Bailey talked to me about it and, in a few days, we had amassed a crew of willing police officers who pledged off-duty time to do the necessary work on Ms.

Jackson's home. They also offered whatever material we could afford, beg, or borrow. Just to make it livable, a contractor told me it would take approximately $6,500. We had the manpower, but that was a lot of money.

On April 27, 1974, the Austin American-Statesman ran a story about the house and soon the citizens of Austin and building contractors responded with materials and expertise in building. Officer Larry Stafford was the contact person at APD. A lot of officers spent their days off working on the project. It was very rewarding for all of us to see someone be as proud and happy as Ms. Jackson was with her "new" house.

Character is revealed by what we do in secret. Officers who worked on this project had only one thing in mind – making Ms. Jackson's home livable. Sgt. Bailey later became Travis County Sheriff.

Officer Foils Holdup—Two Shot

One day I received a "robbery in progress" call at Jacobson Jewelry Store in the 2900 block of West Anderson Lane. Almost immediately, I heard Officer Ronnie Potts go out at that location. On my arrival, I saw Sgt. Darrell Gambrell outside the jewelry store and heard shotgun blasts. As Gambrell and I entered the store, we saw that two people had been shot.

This is what happened: A crook from Dallas named Joe McAller had tried to rob the store. He had locked one employee in the safe and had shot the owner of the store in the leg. As Officer Potts entered the store, the owner of the store stood between Potts and the robber who had a gun in his hand. The owner fell to the floor and Potts shot and wounded the robber with his 12-gauge. The owner of the store was treated and released. The robber was admitted to Brackenridge Hospital and later charged with aggravated robbery with a deadly weapon.

Officer Potts' response time was so good he was stopping in front of the store while the call was going out. In a twist to this incident, a KVUE TV film crew had left the jewelry store only 15 minutes earlier. They had been doing a story on gold prices.

The follow-up investigation showed the robber had taken a shot at Potts. The bullet hit one of the store windows beside where Potts was standing. Potts' reactions were great. He encountered a robbery in progress and correctly did what he had been trained to do.

So many times, a police officer gets a false alarm call. It is easy to let your guard down, but I always told my troops, "Treat all alarm calls as if they are real and dangerous."

Ronnie was a very good, fun-loving officer. His reaction to the situation most likely prevented others from getting shot. The robber had already shot one person and clearly was ready to shoot it out with the police.

Blind Drunk

I responded to a "pedestrian in the roadway" call at the intersection of West 6th Street and Lamar, a high-traffic area. When I got there, I saw that traffic had come to a stop in all directions. People were out of their cars hollering at a pedestrian who was staggering around in the middle of the intersection.

As I started walking toward him, I observed he had a blind person's cane and he was, in fact, blind and drunk.

When I approached him, asking if I could help him, he started swinging the cane in my direction and telling me to "Get the hell away from me or I will beat the crap out of you." As I circled him, he would swing the cane in the direction of my voice. By now, numerous people had gotten out of their cars to watch the show.

The blind drunk was mad and not going anywhere. He knew how to curse and was doing an excellent job of it. It seemed to me like the people watching were more in support of the blind drunk than me. I thought about tackling him, but I didn't want to get him hurt. What I really wanted to do was charge him, whack him with my nightstick, and cuff him. But, that was not my style and it wasn't going to happen.

By now, my backup had arrived. I backed off and we made a plan. Meanwhile, the drunk continued to swing his cane in the direction of my voice. The plan: I would talk to him and my backup would come up behind him and grab him. It worked. We got him cuffed without him getting hurt. At this point, the crowd of people gave a big cheer. I don't know if it was for the blind drunk or for the cops. He was taken to the state school for the blind, still mad and still cursing.

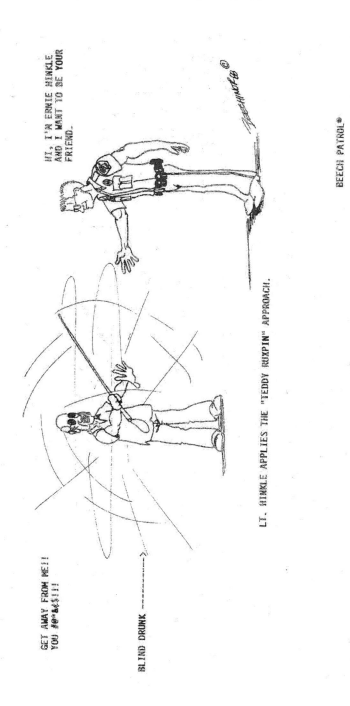

Ernie Hinkle

Importance of a Supportive Family

On June 7, 1980, I married a beautiful lady, Elizabeth Mae Ruede. She is most likely one of the best things that has ever happened to me. Beth had been married before and had two children—Tische was 11 and Donovan was 8 at the time. I raised them as my own and they are a joy in my life. Now responsible adults, they are very special to me.

They are now both married—Tische married Todd Smith who is now an Austin Police lieutenant and they have two sons, Jake and Jackson. Donovan has one son, Nicholas. Together we have seven grandchildren and what a blessing they are to us, and so much fun to be with. Out of the seven, we have six grandsons and only one granddaughter--and, who do you think the boss is?

Beth and I have now been married for 34 years and she has put up with all the many things a police officer's wife has to deal with. After all my years of shift work, mostly working nights, weekends, and holidays and on call-back status, she has always been supportive of me. In fact, without her help and support, it would have been difficult for me to have handled some of the situations I got involved in.

The spouse of a police officer plays an important part in the police officer's job. They live with the fact that when the officer walks out the door, they may never see them alive again. As a first-line supervisor and as I have previously said, usually the last thing I would tell the officers at the end of each roll call was, "Remember, the most important thing you have to do tonight is go home in the morning." Either during or on my watch from 1964 through 1989, seven APD officers did not go home to their families at the end of their shifts. That is something you never get over. Those officers were:

• 1964 - Donald Eugene Carpenter, 28, shot in the head by a burglar.

- 1966 - Billy Paul Speed, 22, shot by sniper, Charles Whitman, who killed 16 and injured 31 when he opened fire from the top of the UT Tower.
- 1974 - Tomas Wayne Bertrong, 31, killed in a collision while responding to back up an officer.
- 1975 - Leland Dale Anderson, 26, shot with his own weapon while questioning three men who attacked him and took his gun.
- 1978 - Ralph Ablanado, 26, was shot with a Russian-made automatic rifle by David Powell after a traffic stop.
- 1989 - Robert Townes Martinez, Jr., was responding to a "shots fired" call. He hit a tree while swerving to miss a vehicle.

Twenty-one APD officers have been killed in the line of duty through April 2012.

Spouses and family members of police officers should be given much credit for their support. I was blessed that my wife and family always supported me. In fact, if it had not been for my wife pushing me, I would have never written this book of my experiences as a police officer. She made it happen.

Finally, the City of Austin, the Austin Police Association, and the citizens of Austin do a great job in supporting the men and women of APD. They have the best equipment that can be afforded, in-service training, and frequent updates on new laws and procedures. When an officer is killed or injured, the officers pull together to take care of that officer's family. The Austin Police Department has and always will be a "family."

Police Burnout

Job burnout is a common problem in most--if not all--professions from medicine to law enforcement. Someone asked me one time how I dealt with burnout as a police officer. I had to think about that. At times, I did feel sorry for myself for having to go to work on a Saturday night, leaving my family when it seemed everyone else was going home. In some cases, I think burnout occurs because police never stop dealing with problems. Things can get out of balance since it's hard for an officer to be able to step back and take a philosophical view of the world.

When I began police work, I had no prejudices. But for three-and-a-half decades, it seemed like all I did was handle problems and that began to wear on me.

In most cases, when a police officer receives a call, the complainant has a problem. If not, they wouldn't be requesting an officer. So cops usually see people at their worst. They may have run a red light or gotten behind the wheel when they were drunk, or they've been injured in a traffic crash, stabbed by a drinking buddy, shot by a stranger, or committed a terrible crime themselves. The list of possibilities goes on and on, but the impact on an officer is the same. It's a stressful job, despite its rewards, and if you don't watch it, your view can get out of perspective.

Almost as a defense, cops start associating only with other cops because they want to get away from the problems and don't want to hear one more civilian tell one more story about a cop who was a butt hole. However, by always being with other cops, they are never very far from work. The world can start looking like everyone but cops are crooks, and cops never stop being cops—not even when they retire.

Most cops don't even like to talk about their life as a cop after retirement. But it is a whole identity and one not easily given up. And, within that identity, I never got over my internal expectations that if I could just work a little harder, I could solve more problems or somehow better protect our citizens.

So, while there were the issues I just described, I can't say I ever experienced burnout. Not much is routine in police work, and that keeps you from getting bored. In fact, at times it was hard to leave my work behind when I left the police station.

To succeed in police work, it is important to be a good listener. It also helps to be humble. It is important to have friends outside of police work. Finally, a cop needs a wishbone, a backbone, and a funny bone.

The 1981 Memorial Day Flood

It had been raining for a few days in Austin but, on Sunday night, Memorial Day 1981, the bottom fell out. Several neighborhoods were totally flooded. The worst hit areas were along Shoal Creek in North Austin to the western edge of downtown.

Our platoon was working the night shift. It was difficult to move around the city due to high water covering so many of the streets. Boats would have been better than our police cars. The Fire Department, Street and Bridge Department, and the Electric Department were doing the best they could to get people to safety.

I was in the 1300 block of North Lamar in front of House Park Stadium stopping traffic until we could get barricades put up. Shoal Creek just west of Lamar had flooded over North Lamar at Park Way Street flooding the roadway with six to eight feet of water going south at a fast flow. At the intersection of 12th and Lamar, water was almost up to the traffic light, taking vehicles and anything not tied down with it. Numerous vehicles and a huge amount of debris washed into Town Lake (now Lady Bird Lake).

Just south of West 5th Street, I was approached by resident, Mr. Clark Covert. He was very concerned about his Ridgelea neighborhood. Bull Creek runs through that neighborhood and was out of its banks. This area is not far from Camp Mabry off MoPac and the 1800 block of West 35th Street. In patrolling the area, I saw that several homes were flooded and some of the residents had to be moved out.

The next day water began to recede and we began to get looting calls in the areas where flooding occurred. We set up a close night patrol of the area. Sgt. Sam Cox, Officers Joe Maciel, Mike Lumas, and Bobby Jones, along with others, did a good job protecting the area until the residents could move back in.

This flood was devastating to Austin. Thirteen people died, eleven of whom had been in their cars. Property loss was astronomical.

Some good did come from this catastrophe. Within the first year after the flood, the City of Austin created an emergency operations center and looked at other ways to improve safety during a flood. Millions of dollars were invested in flood control projects, detention ponds, and floodwalls. The city also developed an extensive early flood warning system.

Austin residents are safer from floods these days, but we live in Central Texas, one of the most flash flood prone areas in the nation. Austinites must always be on the lookout for flood dangers when it rains hard.

City Councilman Shoots a Water Hose

One day in August 1982, Sgt. Ken Mathers radioed for me to meet him at the intersection of Hartford and Niles Road. When I got there, he said there had been a "shots fired" report at an apartment in the 1800 block of Niles Road. Someone had heard shots as they were driving by.

When we checked the apartment, we found Councilman Richard Goodman standing in a doorway holding a .30-30 rifle. He immediately handed it to officers. Goodman seemed excited and confused, though very polite. He said he had been shooting at a snake. We found several spent rounds in the apartment with holes along the baseboards and two in the ceiling. He took us outside where he had shot up a water hose and a tire on his car.

About that time, I began to suspect that Goodman was on cocaine. I had some experience with people using cocaine, and they often saw things that weren't there. In walking back through the apartment, I observed a small amount of hashish, marijuana and a smoking pipe lying on a table. The pipe had no residue in it and the marijuana and hashish were only trace amounts.

I had some decisions to make as to what we were going to do, knowing we had to do something. I didn't feel good about the legality of being in Goodman's apartment, so I let the small amount of drugs alone. We did seize a lever-action Winchester .30-30, a Remington 12-guage semi-automatic shotgun, and 19 spent .30-30 cartridges from Goodman's apartment.

Meanwhile, the young council member was still trying to convince us he had been shooting at a snake. I knew Goodman needed help. It was obvious he had been shooting up the place, but we did not have a witness who saw him shooting.

I asked Goodman if I could help him or take him anywhere. He said he would like to go home to his wife on Pease Road. That was good news for me. I thought the best thing that could be done was to release him to someone who could get him medical attention. I knew I would be criticized for not arresting him, but for what? He could be arrested later if need be. My thinking as an officer was to always put people's safety first—it made no difference who they were.

Goodman had been elected to the city council in 1977 and was well known throughout the city. I took him to his residence on Pease Road. On the way he told me he was glad he wasn't an alcoholic because alcohol was too easy to get. He said God gave him two things—a great memory and a great voice. He thanked me for the way I was treating him. I had talked with him several times in the past, but never under circumstances like these.

When I arrived at his home, I went in with him to meet his wife, Diana. She was a nice lady and was very concerned about her husband. I told Mrs. Goodman what had happened and that I felt he was high on drugs and needed help.

"My husband is going through one of the most difficult times in his life," she told me. "His mother just had major surgery for cancer." At that time, Goodman took me in another room. "Ernie," he said, "I want to show you something." In the room was an iron lung with his 11-year-old son in it. "My son practically has to live in this thing," he continued. "He has Werding-Hoffman disease, a gradual deterioration of the muscles. I love my son. It is hard to listen to this machine all the time."

He said he wasn't trying to blame his son's illness for his actions and admitted that he had some problems he had to deal with. He also said that his son's strength was an inspiration to him. The boy had dictated a letter to his mother asking, "Daddy, are you being brave?"

I talked with both Richard and his wife before I left. They were good people trying to deal on their own with the situation life had dealt them. As I was leaving, Mrs. Goodman said she hoped the incident would be played down. "We will get Richard the help he needs," she told me. "I know that he will come through this thing stronger than ever. He loves Austin and everything about this city. He is a great husband and father and he works so very hard."

I told Mrs. Goodman that I would write my incident report, it would go to Chief Dyson and, as far as my investigation was concerned, it was over. I left their home around 7 a.m. telling Mrs. Goodman I would call her around 10 p.m. to see if I could help in any way. When I called her, she said they were okay and, with the help of friends and family, were working on a plan to seek professional help. The problem was bigger than he could handle on his own, she said, and her husband knew he needed help.

I completed my incident report and routed it to the chief. A day or two later I read the story in the American-Statesman written by Mike Cox, one of the best reporters who ever covered the Austin Police Department. Nothing got by Mike. He would dig it out. The headlines of various follow-up stories by other reporters read, "Councilman Plans Leave of Absence," "Goodman Faces Firearm Charge," and, "Austin police will cite City Councilman Richard Goodman for firing a weapon within the city limits..." (That would have been a Class C misdemeanor with a maximum $200 fine.)

Then the American-Statesman ran an editorial pointing a finger at the department saying we had a double standard. In my eyes, this was not a double standard. This was a prime example of the types of situations a street cop faces almost daily and the decisions they must make. I can somewhat understand the editor, Ray Mariotti, questioning our handling of the case since it is a police officer's job to make arrests.

However, there is much more to being a police officer than jailing someone. As a police officer, anytime I felt I could help someone, I would put their well-being first before getting the criminal justice system involved. An arrest could always be made later, and that is what happened in this case. In most cases, when an officer arrives at the scene, it is obvious who is going to jail. In some cases, however, it is not so obvious without further investigation. I pray police officers are never tied down where they can't use good judgment. Things and situations are not always as black and white as they seem. Officers I worked with always tried to do the right thing for everyone.

Goodman had many friends and supporters. In 1980, a poll of Austin residents found Goodman to be the most popular of the council members. He ended up taking a three-week leave of absence from the council and checked himself into Care Manor Hospital in Orange County, CA for drug rehabilitation and medical problems, according to an article in the American-Statesman published September 8, 1982.

The editor visited Goodman and wrote an article headlined, "Richard Goodman's Story: 'a flirtatious kiss with drugs.'" In it, he said: "Goodman was very candid in the interview saying, 'I don't have a thick skin, and I am ultra-sensitive, especially for a politician. That probably helped drive me to drugs'." Goodman also said, "By the way, it was a bum rap you guys gave the Police Department. I've known Lt. (Ernie) Hinkle a long time. He took me home to Diana (Dee-anna) and asked her, 'Is he gonna be all right?' He left me with her and no deals were ever made." He went on to declare: "This is a great Police Department. They've never given me preferential treatment."

Goodman returned to his elected duties clean of drugs and in good humor. The following year he announced he would not run for re-election. He said, "I have a big heart—I just happened to tangle with the devil."

Goodman died in Burbank, CA in 2005. He was 55 and left many friends in Austin. I am proud to say I was one of them.

Snow Storm – Lost Husband

It doesn't snow much in Austin but, when it does, it can cause a lot of problems. On January 12, 1983, I was working the day shift which ended at 3 p.m. It started snowing around noon and, by 2 p.m., the streets had started freezing over. Most employers sent their workers home and schools let students out early.

By the time I left the police station, the roads were very icy and the snow was still coming down. I figured my best route home was to take 15th Street to MoPac. I was traveling west on 15th and saw that traffic had stopped. I took the Lamar Boulevard exit only to see that the roadway was blocked. So there I sat and there I continued to sit. This was well before we had cell phones, and nothing around me was open. A few people were still in their vehicles, like me, but most of the cars had been abandoned.

About 11 p.m., nearly eight hours after I had left for home, several UT students came by. I asked them if they could push me over the curb down a little hill to Lamar. They were eager to help. I was still in my police uniform and they thought it was pretty funny that I was stuck in that situation.

We managed to get my truck on Lamar and I slowly began driving south on Lamar, going the wrong way. I took 6th Street west to MoPac and then headed north. I finally got home about 2 a.m. Boy, did I get a chewing out from my wife. She had called the police department several times talking to Lt. Glen Garrett. Glen told her, "Oh, Ernie is okay. He is out there somewhere trying to get home."

Not only did I have to deal with Beth but, for the next week or so, my troops delighted in bringing me all kinds of bad weather survival kits.

"Hit Him Where It Hurts"

I received a call to check on a lady who lived alone on Owen Street just east of the 3500 block of North Lamar. On my arrival, I talked to a Mrs. Ora Gibson who was about 70. She said she was fine, but wanted me to have a glass of tea with her.

While we drank tea on her back porch, Mrs. Gibson said, "I want you to do something for me. I want you to take my BB gun and shoot a squirrel for me. They are getting my pecans from my two trees."

I said, "Mrs. Gibson, it is against the law to shoot BB guns in the city." She said, "I know. But, my eyesight is bad and I can't hit them anymore."

She had a big back yard with two big pecan trees. She said, "I never kill them–I just run them off." I didn't see any harm in shooting up in the trees, so I took her little spring-powered Red Rider BB gun and went squirrel hunting. In a little bit, I saw a big squirrel sitting on a limb. I was about to shoot when Mrs. Gibson said, "I want you to shoot him in the balls so he won't come back." Trying hard to keep from laughing, I didn't shoot that accurately, but the squirrel ran off after I pulled the trigger.

As time permitted, I would go by Mrs. Gibson's home every week to have tea with her. This is a memo I got from Chief Dyson's office in 1985:

> "Message to Lt. Hinkle:
> Chief Frank Dyson wants you personally to contact this lady and obtain the information from her and then report back to him. She will only talk to Lt. Hinkle and no one else in the Dept."

Mrs. Gibson had a neat and very clean home. She and her late husband had bought the house back in the late 1930s when that area was considered to be in the country. Her husband would ride a horse to town. With her husband gone, she didn't trust many people, but she trusted me. She started to want to give me things. I refused to take anything and it upset her. She had an old oil lamp she wanted me to have. She called the chief and got permission for me to take it. I still have that lamp and it is one of my prized possessions.

You couldn't help but become friends with Mrs. Gibson. She was a sweet old lady. Once when I was off duty, my family and I went by and took her to dinner at Luby's Cafeteria.

Sometime later, I stopped to visit her and she said, "Ernie, I want to show you something." She took me in her bedroom, pulled the mattress back, and it was loaded with money. She said, "I don't believe in banks, so I keep my money under my mattress and sleep on it." I said, "Mrs. Gibson, I wish you hadn't shown me that money. It is not safe there. Anything could happen. You need to put it in a bank." She would have no part of that. I was very concerned. It looked like a lot of money.

There was a bank at North Lamar and 38th Street. One day I stopped in there and talked to the bank president. I told him about my situation without naming anyone. He said he would be glad to help anyone become trusting of his bank. I began talking to Mrs. Gibson about how worried I was about her keeping that money under her mattress. I asked her if I could take her to the bank closest to her so she could just talk to them. She finally said okay. We went to the bank and the banker went over everything with her. After we left, I asked her if the banker could come to her house so she could get to know him. "That would be okay," she said. After taking her home, I went back and talked to the banker and he went with me back to her house which was only about four blocks. I left him with her.

The banker went by to see her every week for a month or so. He got her confidence and it wasn't long before they moved the money to the bank. I don't know how much it was, but the banker told me it was a lot. Mrs. Gibson showed me a statement where she was getting about $120 a month in interest. She would walk up to the bank every week to check on her money. She was happy about having her money in the bank and, believe me, I was relieved.

I don't think I ever hit one of her squirrels in the balls, but we kept them moving.

Working Traffic

A street officer's vehicle, in most cases, is his office. Being in that unit eight to ten hours a day is, in itself, a hazard whether the officer works for the city, county or state. A lot of officers are hurt or killed working traffic around a collision, especially in fast traffic. No matter how many traffic cones or police units are blocking a collision scene, it is still dangerous.

Officer Drew Alan Bolin, 25, was killed by a drunk driver while working a collision on IH-35. Drew had done everything he could to protect himself. Officer Clinton Hunter, 22, was killed in 1995 by a drunk driver while rolling out a stinger. A stinger is a strip of spikes positioned across a roadway to stop a fleeing vehicle. Several times at collision scenes I had to dive out of the path of a vehicle that would have run over me.

Early in my career I worked on a special collision investigation unit, mostly only handling wrecks on and around IH-35, city limit to city limit. I could drive IH-35 through the city and, within about every mile, could remember a fatal collision. Speed and lack of attention on the driver's part seemed to be the common denominator. It is not a pretty sight to see a deceased person in a vehicle knowing their family will get the sad and devastating news soon.

A collision I investigated around 7:30 a.m. on a drizzly Friday morning in the 1900-2100 blocks of IH-35 on the southbound lower deck involved the most vehicles I ever saw in one accident. Arriving at the scene, I saw vehicles scattered everywhere. Some were completely turned around and facing oncoming traffic. People were out of their cars and walking around all over the roadway. I was thinking, "What in the heck am I going to do?"

As I walked up after I got out of my unit, people began to crowd around me. The first thing I did was ask if anyone was injured. One driver had a bloody nose and two ladies said they had whiplash, but all refused treatment. I told everyone to return to their cars and have their driver's licenses and insurance cards ready. I then walked about a two-block area checking all the vehicles.

The rain had left the roadway slicker than owl crap. Thirty-eight vehicles had been involved in the chain-reaction accident. It took five wreckers to haul off all the cars that couldn't be driven. Officers had re-routed traffic off the expressway and I called for another officer to assist me in getting all drivers' information. Sgt. Mark Cutler came to help me and promptly ran into the back of my parked unit. Fortunately, there was no damage to either unit.

I started getting driver information at the initial point of impact on the southern end of the scene, and Mark started on the northern end. After getting all the required information, I let them go if their vehicle was drivable. Most of the vehicles just had fender-bender damage. It took us about two and a half hours to investigate the accident, and the roadway stayed closed for about three hours. In the end, we decided not to file charges due to weather conditions.

That accident took a lot of time to sort out, but investigating fatal collisions was always a tougher job. Street officers, like homicide investigators do for murder victims, try to do the best job we can for the deceased. Focusing on those who had died also helped me in staying motivated.

One time in the 3700 block of the lower deck of IH-35, a rear wheel came off an 18-wheeler. The big tire bounced around and crashed through the windshield on the driver's side of a southbound vehicle killing the driver.

Another day, about 7 a.m., I received a call about a minor collision in the 6500 block of IH-35 northbound. I was going north on the frontage road as traffic began slowing to a stop on the expressway in about the 4900 block northbound. About then, I got a call about another collision. I was within two blocks of that one and went to it first. Two 18-wheelers hauling gravel were involved. The first one slowed for traffic, but the one following didn't have time to stop and ran into the back of the stopped truck. As a result, the weight of the gravel in the back truck transferred the load through the cab of the front truck pinning the driver against the steering wheel and dashboard of the cab. Just as I arrived, the front truck caught on fire.

We tried to free the driver, but the door wouldn't open and he couldn't move. As it turned out, the driver in the back truck was the father of the young man trapped in his truck. By now, the flames were engulfing him. He called out, "Please don't let me burn up." The fire extinguisher I had didn't do anything to squelch the fire.

Meanwhile, his father was still trying to get him out. But the flames grew so intense that we couldn't get close to him anymore. He begged for me to shoot him, screaming, "Don't let me burn up." By now, fire trucks had arrived. We had to physically subdue his father who had suffered serious burns on his face, hands, and arms trying to rescue his son. It didn't take firefighters long to knock down the blaze, but it was too late for the young man who had been trapped in the truck. When the coroner moved the body, it had shriveled up to where it could have been put in a paper sack.

Don't think I didn't consider shooting him to get him out of his horrible pain. In fact, I did unsnap my gun, but by then he had stopped crying for help and the fire had completely engulfed the cab. If the fire had not spread so quickly to the point where I could no longer see him, to keep him from burning alive, I know I would have shot him and turned in my badge. When I left the scene, I went to a nearby back alley and cried like a baby. You never get over something like that.

Wife Sees Husband Die in Wreck

Collisions take only a matter of seconds. If we could back up only 20 seconds, most crashes could be prevented.

One morning in 1982, an elderly Austin man was killed when a truck broadsided his car at a North Austin intersection. The man's wife, who was following behind him in another car, witnessed the collision and saw her husband die. This occurred at the intersection of Wilshire and Airport Boulevards.

Ernie Hinkle

The couple had been on their way to gas up their cars. The husband stopped for a stop sign, but apparently didn't see the oncoming truck and pulled right out in front of it. The force of the collision knocked his 1974 Lincoln Continental about half a block south of the intersection. The truck driver was not hurt.

It fell on me to tell the wife that her husband was dead. We comforted her as best we could, helped her get home, and got Victim Services with her.

Looking for Santa Claus

Christmas is a special time of the year for most people. But it is easy to get away from the real meaning of Christmas—the birth of Jesus—and go gift-shopping crazy.

About 11 a.m. on Christmas Eve in 1982, I was working the streets along with Capt. Spohnholtz when we got a disturbance call at the Bel Air Motel on South Congress Avenue. Finding the room where the disturbance was coming from, we saw several Christmas presents scattered in the hallway adjacent to the room. We could hear loud noises--cursing and laughing-- coming from inside the room. When I knocked on the door and said, "Police!" the noises stopped and a male voice said, "Come on in." As we went in, we saw three transients.

"We are here legally," one of them said. "The Salvation Army put us up here for a week during Christmas."

"What is the deal with the Christmas packages in the hallway?" I asked.

"Somebody dropped them off for us and there isn't a damn bit of alcohol or beer in them and we don't want them," he answered.

"Santa Claus could have left them," I said, kidding him.

"You have got to be the craziest SOB I have ever seen or heard of," he said. "Have you ever heard of Mensa International? I am in the top 98 percent of the highest IQ people in the United States. I am so damn smart that I am crazy. For you to

[182]

suggest there is a Santa Claus is like telling me the cow jumped over the moon."

"Well, sir," I replied. "I am not as smart as you are, but I do believe in Santa Claus. I just saw him out in North Austin about two hours ago."

At first, he shook his head and looked at me like I was crazy. He then started laughing along with the other men in the room. Soon we were all laughing and wishing each other a Merry Christmas.

Capt. Spohnholtz and I thought about going and buying them a case of beer for Christmas, but better judgment prevailed.

Usually we were very busy on Christmas Day. Some families had been together too long and started having problems with each other and some people didn't like what they got for Christmas. I have seen turkeys thrown into fireplaces and Christmas trees tossed on top of houses by people who suddenly fell out of the holiday spirit.

On top of that, the day after Christmas is depressing to a lot of people. It seems it is such a letdown after leading up to the celebrations of Christmas. I remember making several suicide calls just after Christmas.

For our family, however, Christmas was always a pleasure. We celebrated the birth of our Lord, exchanged gifts as a family, shared our love for each other, ate good food, and still believed in Santa Claus. What a wonderful thing it is to have a loving family and just be together.

Working Halloween Nights on East 6th Street

Officers working East 6th Street on Halloween nights really earn their salaries. Starting in the afternoon, the downtown street is closed to vehicle traffic from Congress Avenue east to IH-35. Barricades are placed in the center lanes leaving the officers a 10 to 12-foot space to move up and down the street. Costumed pedestrians then take over the street walking on the outsides of the barricades. We would have around 50 officers working the downtown area trying to prevent crimes with a show of force so our citizens could have a good time and enjoy themselves.

I believe it was Halloween night in 1985 that Sr. Sgt. Dell Shaw was behind the barricades in the 100 block of the street when someone threw a five to six-foot plant at Dell from the balcony of the second or third floor of the Driskill Hotel. The heavy plant only missed him by a foot or two. Dell saw people running on the balcony, but didn't see who threw the plant. A short time later, someone came up to Dell saying he was with the Driskill Hotel and wanted the plant back. Dell wouldn't let him have it—he didn't want it thrown at him again. Not wanting to take no for an answer, the Driskill employee started around the barricades to get the tree when Officer Pat Andrews put him back over the barricades.

I soon received a call about the incident from someone with the Driskill security staff. I told him that if the hotel could help us identify who threw the plant, we would release it back to them. Until then, it would be kept for evidence.

I don't remember what happened to the plant. I just know Dell was some hacked off about it and it wasn't thrown at him anymore.

Dell was one of the best officers I ever worked with. He was Adam Sector's northwest senior sergeant on our platoon and a good leader. He was always right there on a call with his officers. When Dell got promoted to lieutenant, as much as I was happy for him, I hated to see him leave our shift. It is hard to replace a leader like that.

Lt. Shaw was later elected president of the Austin Police Association. Between him and outgoing president, Sgt. Jerry Spain, they accomplished much in getting better working conditions and better pay for APD. I am proud to call Dell Shaw (now retired) my friend.

Pursuits

There is no safe way to chase a car, but sometimes a police officer has no choice but to pursue a vehicle. I hated pursuits and would call them off anytime circumstances would allow.

In the 1990s, APD's pursuit policy was that only two units would be involved in a chase—the first unit and one backup unit to handle the radio communications. Other units could be involved if it was a known felony stop.

One example was when an officer called in that he would be out of his unit on a disturbance call in the parking lot of the Seven-Eleven Store at Koenig Lane and North Lamar Boulevard. Moments later, he radioed that he would be in pursuit of a stolen red Volkswagen going west on Koenig. The chase then turned north on Grover where the red Volkswagen finally pulled over. As the officer approached the driver, he took off again. By the time the officer could run back to his unit, the red car had run a stop sign at the intersection of Grover and Justin Lane and hit an Oldsmobile. Seven people in the Oldsmobile were injured, including an infant girl who was in critical condition and not expected to live. All the rest were in serious condition.

Four juveniles were in the stolen car—three 15-year-olds and one 11-year-old—all went to the hospital in fair condition. In all, 11 people had been hurt. Back at the Seven-Eleven, I found out the car had been stolen from there. One of the attendants had made an effort to stop the car and the driver tried to run him over. The chase had lasted less than a mile.

I remember my first pursuit back in early 1961. We were working the night shift. At that time, only about eight officers were working nights. One of the officers called in that he was trying to stop a vehicle for a traffic violation and he would be in pursuit going north from the 1500 block of Red River.

As it happened, I was in the 1900 block of Red River and fell in behind the passing police car. We went west on 19th Street (now MLK), then north on Guadalupe. On Guadalupe, we picked up two more police units going about 60 mph. The car we were chasing continued out North Lamar where two more police units got in the chase. We now had six police units in a parade trying to pass each other to get to the car we were chasing.

Going west on U.S. 183 headed out of the city, my unit got a hot radiator hose, so I had to pull out. Then the motor went out on another officer's car. A third unit had to leave the chase when a tire went flat. Not to miss out on the action, the officer changed the tire and got back into the chase. Still another officer involved in the pursuit had a minor collision when he hit an animal in the roadway.

The chase finally ended just outside of Cedar Park when the motor blew up on the vehicle we had been chasing. One Austin officer and a DPS trooper arrested the subject at the location for eluding an officer.

Six of the eight officers covering the city had been involved in the chase. When he got the report, Chief Miles was not happy. Soon we had written guidelines to follow in chases.

Pursuits are hazardous for everyone. It puts the citizens in harm's way and police officers in danger, as well.

Complaint Against Officers Serving a Felony Warrant

Police officers sometimes get criticized simply for doing their jobs. Don't misunderstand—officers do make mistakes. Cops are humans, too.

Over my many years in law enforcement, I have investigated a lot of complaints against police officers. The majority of the time the cases proved to be unfounded. Even so, our citizens have a right to complain. If an officer has screwed up, there is no place for that and corrective action should be taken.

In February 1987, I received a complaint from a woman about the way some of the officers in my platoon handled the arrest of her son at her house in Northeast Austin. She said she told the officers that her son wasn't there, but that they came into her house anyway knocking over a baby's highchair with the baby in it, breaking some furniture, and pushing members of her family around. The woman also told me that she had a heart problem and almost had a heart attack during the incident. She wanted something done to the officers involved.

Shortly after taking her complaint, I contacted Sr. Sgt. Manuel Peña. He told me that his sector had tracked down the woman's son who had two felony warrants for burglary, two additional felony cases pending in court and eight assorted traffic warrants. Suspecting that the subject was staying at his mother's house, the sergeant left a photograph with neighbors and told them to call police if they saw the guy.

After obtaining good information that the wanted man was indeed at his mother's house, Sgt. Manuel Peña, along with Officers Dennis Clark, Michael Larner, and Todd Myers went to serve the felony warrants. When they got there, the sergeant told the mother that they had felony arrest warrants for her son and to send him out.

The mother said her son was not at home and told the officers to leave. However, based on what they had been told by neighbors, the officers believed the suspect was in the house and forcibly entered the residence to serve the warrants. They had been immediately confronted by the mother who continued to deny that her boy was in the house. Again, she told them to leave.

At that point, in her agitated state, the mother—not an officer—accidentally ran into a high chair with a baby in it. Officer Dennis Clark picked the baby up and handed it to another woman in the room. Several other children were in the house and the suspect's mother told them to hit the officers. With no help from any family members, the officers found the suspect hiding in the attic and took him into custody.

After following up on the woman's complaint, I went to her residence to tell her what I had come up with in my investigation, which was quite different from what she had told me. Actually, the officers at the house had shown considerable restraint in dealing with the family members.

I said that I was sorry her son had to be arrested at her home, but that I also didn't feel she had been honest with the officers. That had added to the problem. As a mother, she really had not been protecting her son by lying to the police.

Angry Sergeant

Sgt. Manuel Peña was supervisor over Charlie Sector in East Austin, usually our busiest sector. He was a hard working leader making every backup call he could.

I backed him up on a silent burglary alarm call about 2 a.m. one morning in the 1300 block of East 12th Street. When I got there, Peña had eight subjects lined up against the east side of the building and he was clearly angry about something. I soon found out while he had been checking the interior of the building, someone had stolen equipment from his police car. He was reading the riot act to them, demanding to know where his police gear was.

I saw a dumpster behind the building and walked back to check it. I had learned a long time before that dumpsters magically seem to attract evidence. And there it was—Pena's clipboard and other city equipment.

Meanwhile, after the sergeant told everyone he had rounded up that he was going to arrest them for theft, they began to talk and finally fingered the person who took the equipment. In the end, no one got arrested. As a result, the sergeant earned the trust of a good street contact who gave him useful information as time went on.

I enjoyed working with Manuel. You always knew he was on top of things and his officers took on his personality and work ethic.

Ice on the Roadway

When the first ice storm hit after the upper deck of IH-35 was completed and opened for traffic, the State Highway Department called APD and said they were closing the upper deck because it would be too hazardous for vehicle traffic. The shutdown started about 4 p.m.

I was working the night shift from 11 p.m. to 7 a.m. It had been sleeting and raining during the day—now it was just a dry, cold night. About 1 a.m., after driving all over the city, Austin seemed to be locked down. Nothing was moving on the streets. I decided I would see if the upper deck was really all that dangerous. In fact, I didn't think that it should have been closed in the first place.

I drove around the barricades going north, slowly going up the ramp. When I reached where the roadway leveled out, my unit began to slide sideways almost hitting the west concrete wall. I started to get out of the car, but couldn't get my door open because it was too close to the wall.

I was doing some serious thinking at this point trying to figure how I was going to get out of there and praying I wouldn't get a hot call while I was stuck. I really didn't want to radio for help.

I exited the right side of my unit and found the roadway so slick I couldn't even stand up unless I held on to the car. I walked around the car and got between the car and the wall. I thought about just walking off the upper deck by clinging to the wall, but quickly ruled that out. I really didn't want anyone to know what I had gotten myself into.

I checked the trunk of the car hoping the police garage might have put some chains in there, but no such luck. I saw that if I got against the wall, I could move the vehicle by pushing it with my feet. I moved the vehicle over enough to open the driver's door, then got inside to warm up.

Sitting there, I came up with a plan. Since the ice made it easy enough to move a vehicle, I would push my car off the upper deck. I rolled down the driver's door window, turned the engine off, got out and began to push. That worked well enough until the vehicle got away from me and slid about 40 yards as I held on to the door for dear life. Fortunately, I was able to get it stopped.

After about three and one-half hours of working in the cold, I got the vehicle to a point where I could drive it off.

Right then was when I vowed that I would never again question the judgment of the Texas Highway Department.

Larry Cowie was the department's Austin area maintenance supervisor. A few weeks later, I told him what I had done and he often kidded me about it. I never said anything to the officers I worked with. At Show-down later that night, someone asked me where I had been all shift. I answered that I had been catching up on paperwork. I did confess what I had done to Capt. Spohnholtz who said he wasn't one bit surprised.

Alien Abduction

Cold weather is a great crime fighter. One freezing night In December 1993, I was working the night shift. Since it was so slow, Sgt. Greg Lasley called and asked if I wanted to ride with him and that seemed like a good idea.

We patrolled downtown and the UT area. There was no traffic moving and the radio was quiet. All businesses had been closed due to the hazardous weather.

To have some fun, I asked Greg if he had ever been to outer space. He looked at me a little funny and said that he had been to the Space Center in Houston. "That's not what I mean," I said. "I'm talking about outer space!" "No! Have you?" Greg asked. "Yep," I replied with a straight face, and started telling him in great detail about the time I had been abducted by aliens and taken into their spaceship. I told him the people on board looked like small robots. They had only one eye, no ears, hands with only one finger, and a flexible antenna coming out of their heads. I really got into it and Greg started looking at me as if I had gone nuts.

But I kept going! I told him, "They took me to Mars by way of Venus and time just seemed to stand still. In fact, I learned that one year of space-time equals roughly 30 Earth years. The aliens were good to me and mostly ignored me, other than putting wires all over my body and playing with my ears; and, the lights on the ship were constantly changing colors and the changing of the lights seemed to have some control over the performance of the ship. I could feel the ship moving—probably at the rate of Mach 1 or more."

I was so into my practical joke that I wasn't paying any attention to our location. All of a sudden, Greg pulled into the State Hospital at 4110 Guadalupe and headed directly to the admissions office, a place I had taken many a troubled person.

"What are we doing here?" I asked.

"Ernie," he said with a serious look on his face, "this is where aliens are debriefed."

By this time, white-coated attendants were coming out to the police car to meet us in case we needed help with the person being committed.

I pulled rank and told Greg to get my butt out of there and take me back to my car.

When word of my backfired gag spread among the troops, within a few days I had been presented with a "True Believer's Award" and the "Veteran of Alien Spaceship Ride Award." Copies of my certificates were posted all over the station.

Greg, a sharp officer who soon got promoted to lieutenant, had gotten the last laugh <u>twice</u>.

Ernie Hinkle

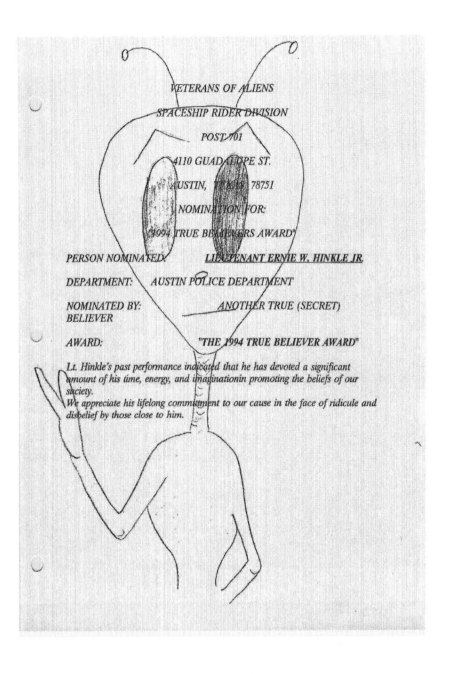

VETERANS OF ALIENS

SPACESHIP RIDER DIVISION

POST 701

4110 GUADALUPE ST.

AUSTIN, TEXAS 78751

NOMINATION FOR:

"1994 TRUE BELIEVERS AWARD"

PERSON NOMINATED: LIEUTENANT ERNIE W. HINKLE JR.

DEPARTMENT: AUSTIN POLICE DEPARTMENT

NOMINATED BY: ANOTHER TRUE (SECRET)
BELIEVER

AWARD: "THE 1994 TRUE BELIEVER AWARD"

Lt. Hinkle's past performance indicated that he has devoted a significant amount of his time, energy, and imagination in promoting the beliefs of our society.
We appreciate his lifelong commitment to our cause in the face of ridicule and disbelief by those close to him.

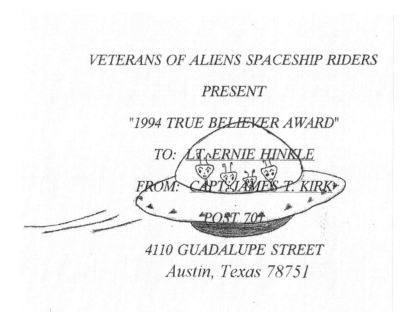

VETERANS OF ALIENS SPACESHIP RIDERS

PRESENT

"1994 TRUE BELIEVER AWARD"

TO: LT. ERNIE HINKLE

FROM: CAPT. JAMES T. KIRK

POST 701

4110 GUADALUPE STREET
Austin, Texas 78751

Frozen Water?

Early one morning, Capt. Bill Pence called me at Show-up and said that Sgt. Lasley had called to say that he would be late for work because the water at his house had frozen during the night. It was around the first of November, about 48 degrees, and we hadn't had a freeze in Austin since the previous winter.

As it turned out, somebody had turned Greg's water off at the meter during the night. When Greg finally got to work and explained this, he said he had a suspect and looked at me pretty hard. I had no comment.

Ernie Hinkle

Family Seeks a Court Order

Sgt. Lasley married a beautiful lady, Cheryl Johnson. An attorney, Cheryl would knit blankets and socks and give them to the needy around Christmas time.

In 1995, I needed a good attorney and asked Cheryl if she would take my case. She agreed and we went over the facts: When three of my grandchildren, Brittney, Travis, and Coby, were young (8 to 10), I started taking them to Hooters--which I claimed was just a family restaurant--for burgers and a big screen TV. Grandson Corey, being only four years old at the time, didn't get to see the large screen TV at Hooters until he was about nine or ten years old, but he was equally impressed when one of the waitresses came over and sat with us for a while.

All went well until Brittney told her parents that Papaw took them to Hooters. They didn't like it and called a family meeting.

My son, Ricky, a police officer himself, got a judge to sign a "court order" that I wasn't adult enough to be with the grandchildren alone and was grounded from taking them any-where without supervision for six months. Cheryl threw me under the bus, siding with my family.

Cheryl Johnson now sits on the Third Court of Criminal Appeals and clearly is an impartial jurist. As my friend, she sure didn't cut me any slack.

End of a Tradition

When a police officer got a promotion from Patrolman I to Patrolman II, usually after two years, it was customary for the sergeant to pin on his or her new badge at Show-up or roll call. It was also customary that once the badge had been pinned on, the sergeant would slap it pretty hard for good luck.

After performing this ceremony one night, Greg came to my office saying he thought his wrist was broken. I told him to go have it checked. He went to Brackenridge ER and, sure enough, he had a broken wrist. After about three hours, Greg came back with a cast on his hand.

I wrote it up as an on-the-job injury, but the Safety Board didn't agree with my conclusion. I met with them and explained that the promotional ritual had been a practice for years. The board finally, after a butt chewing, approved it as a work-related injury. However, that put an end to the good luck slap tradition at APD.

Flying the Flag at Police Headquarters

As far back as I could remember, every day about 7 a.m. APD custodian Oliver Houston raised the American flag on the pole in front of the police station. I watched this one morning when I was on the day shift and got the idea for a prank on my good friend, Lt. Ben Vega, who was always stuffing junk in my mailbox at the station.

Deciding it was time for some payback, I waited until Ben went on the day shift which ran from 5 a.m. to 3 p.m. Then I wrote a memo to him under Chief Miles' name asking him to please raise the flag each day during the time he was on the day shift.

The lieutenant was a very conscientious officer. If he was assigned a job, it got done. One day, as Ben and two of his officers were raising the flag, Chief Miles drove up. Puzzled, he told them they were doing a good job, but asked why they were doing it. Ben told the chief he had a memo instructing him to. The chief told him he didn't have to do that anymore, that Oliver would be taking care of it.

Lt. Vega did some counseling with me suspecting that I had forged the chief's signature. About a month later, the chief stopped me in the hallway and told me he was perfectly capable of signing his own memos. Fortunately, he said that with a smile on his face. I never heard any more about it.

Ernie Hinkle

When is a Police Officer Off Duty?

In 1966, I took my son, Ricky, to a basketball game at Gregory Gym on the UT campus. Ricky was about ten years old at the time. We enjoyed going to Texas games when my schedule would permit.

On the way home around 9:30 p.m. driving north on Guadalupe, I stopped for a red light at 45th Street. We were the third vehicle in line. As we sat there waiting for the light to change, I saw a man get out of the vehicle in front of us, slam the door, and run up to the driver's door of the vehicle in front of him. He began cursing and punching the driver, an elderly male. Next thing I knew, this older man opened his car door and came out with a gun. Then a second person in the car in front of us bailed out and ran to the first car to help subdue the elderly man.

All this happened in an instant. There I was with my son. His safety was all I could think about, but the two men knocked the elderly man down and took his gun. I told Ricky to stay in the truck and I got out holding up my badge, yelling "Police!" and "Knock it off!"

The subject with the gun started running east on 45th Street. The other one went west. I took off after the guy with the gun. Pretty soon, I saw him toss the weapon, which made me feel a lot better.

About two blocks into the chase, I caught him. I was one pissed off cop about the way he had treated that old man. On the way back to the scene, I found the gun he had discarded. When I got back to my truck, I was very happy to see Officer Ted Hargis was there.

I checked on my son knowing he was probably scared to death. But Ricky was okay except for the fact that he had been worried about me. He had told Ted that I was after somebody going down 45th Street. He was a very brave boy and I was proud of him. I hated to have put Ricky in that position, but that fight easily could have ended in a shooting.

[196]

I filled Ted in on what had happened and the two men who had accosted the old man got charged with assault. I never knew what started the incident, but suspect it was road rage.

APD general orders at the time said that off-duty officers were not to take action in misdemeanor cases, but that action should be taken in felony or assault cases and in preventing a crime. I never liked getting involved in cases off duty. Most often, it turned into a no-win situation. But if you are a police officer, at times you have no choice when it comes to protecting life or property. I did, at times, arrest a DWI while off duty, but I also turned a blind eye on numerous traffic violations. Anywhere we would go as a family I always kept a low profile, but with my back to the wall just in case.

Another time when I was off duty but had no choice about getting involved was in October 1982, three days before my daughter was getting married to my son-in-law, Greg Baker. Greg's parents, Alice and Hollis Baker, had a rehearsal dinner for the wedding party at a nice restaurant on West Anderson Lane.

As we finished up, a group of about a dozen well-dressed people at another table began getting up. Somehow I missed it, but Hollis told me a man in the party had just slapped a woman. When the other table got up to leave, I followed them outside and saw the guy slap the lady again. I went over, got between them and pushed him against the wall, telling everyone I was a police officer.

The man pushed me back. I didn't have handcuffs so I put him back on the wall a little more forcefully this time. About that time, another member of the party came up and said the young man I had against the wall was his son and that he and his girlfriend were just having a disagreement. The father said his son had been drinking and asked if he could just take him home. I told him his son was going to jail for assault, that there was no excuse for him to be hitting his girlfriend.

I guess someone called for the police because a district officer drove up into the parking lot. The officer and I put the subject in the back of the police car until we could get things sorted out. I talked to his girlfriend who still had a large red spot on her face from being slapped. I asked if she would sign an assault complaint, but she said no. She didn't want him to go to jail. His father said if we would release his son to him, he would get him some help. The guy should have gone to jail, but we released him to his family after he apologized to his girlfriend.

Our dinner had been about over when the disturbance started. I felt bad about what happened since it had diverted attention from my daughter. But Vickie took it in stride and said she was glad we had been there to prevent the lady from being hit again. Hollis Baker had my back, ready to help anyway he could and I really appreciated it.

Melee at 1015 Catalpa

On October 2, 1987, my platoon was working the night shift. Sgt. Gary Richards of the Repeat Offenders Program (ROP Unit) said they would be serving a narcotics search warrant at 1015 Catalpa and requested assistance from uniformed officers. We were very familiar with that address which was a fairly large apartment complex and a dope haven. The police got a lot of calls from there.

The Jamaican's Gang liked to hang out there and we had some information they were involved in a conspiracy to have one of the ROP officers shot. We kept a close patrol of that location as often as we could. I had driven by there several times in the past and had heard shots fired, but had never been able to locate where they came from.

Sometimes, despite all the intelligence we can get, the very best plans turn to crap in a hurry. That is somewhat what happened executing this warrant. Sgt. Richards and his ROP officers met in his office along with Sgt. Manuel Peña, supervisor of Charlie Sector, to work out where each officer would go.

Richards had already posted a plainclothes officer to watch the address and make note of who was coming and going. The plan was that Sgt. Peña would descend on the complex with four officers when the ROP officers hit the place. Peña emphasized to the troops that: (1) this was a high drug dealing area; (2) known criminals lived in and visited the location regularly; and, (3) arrests had been made for carrying guns and knives. Most of the residents of that area were also known to have very little respect for police officers.

The raid would take place at 12:30 a.m. The ROP officers would execute the warrants at two different apartments and the uniformed officers under Peña would assist them by securing the parking lot and blocking the entrance to the complex. Two other sergeants would be there with the paddy wagon to handle multiple arrests. I would be the ranking officer at the scene.

After checking with the lookout at the complex and hearing that all was quiet, we hit the complex at 12:35 a.m. On the initial entry, people came out of the woodwork. Shots were being fired all around the complex and the driver of a vehicle trying to leave the parking lot attempted to run over Officer Aurelio Martinez. Martinez jumped out of the way and Sgt. Ralph DeLa Fuente shot at the vehicle, but the driver got away.

Meanwhile, I heard several more shots as officers struggled with several arrested subjects. Sgt. Richards was being dragged by one subject when another officer assisted in arresting the man. I called for more backup, which we had on standby, and soon got the incident under control.

When the dust settled, 10 people had been arrested for various offenses. Everyone taken into custody had to be subdued–no one at the scene offered any cooperation. Thank God, despite all the shooting, no one got hit. Sgt. Peña checked all the officers' weapons at the scene and found that only two officers had fired their weapons. Each officer had fired one shot at the vehicle that nearly ran over Officer Martinez, a well-justified use of force. Without the high quality of officers involved in this incident, the outcome could have been much different. They were all well-trained, seasoned, and very professional. The only thing I would have done differently was to have the SWAT team present.

The vehicle that tried to run over Martinez was a brown Ford Thunderbird with New Mexico license plates. A "pickup" had been broadcast for officers to be on the lookout for that vehicle. About 4:30 a.m., an officer located the vehicle near Branch and East 1111 Streets. It was occupied by two subjects, Robert and Tiffany Day. The vehicle had damage to the right passenger door where the officer had tried to stop it and on the front where it had hit and pushed away an unmarked police unit. The subjects in the car said they had borrowed the vehicle from someone they left sleeping in his motel room on South Congress.

An officer went to the motel and gave that man an early, in-person, wake-up call. A warrant check showed he had outstanding traffic warrants so he was arrested. Around 5:30 a.m., I interviewed the man and Officer Martinez positively identified him as the driver of the car who attempted to run over him. The man admitted he was the driver of the car, but said he hadn't been trying to hurt the officer. He just wanted to get out of there. He claimed that when he saw police officers and people running everywhere and heard shots being fired, he panicked and accelerated off the parking lot. He denied trying to run over the officer or that he had a gun.

We still filed on the man for aggravated assault on a police officer, but I think he had found himself in the wrong place at the wrong time and just used bad judgment.

Arrest and Release

Thinking back on my early career working the night shift in Baker Sector downtown, I remember one time around 10 p.m. when I was stopped at a traffic light northbound on the East Frontage Road at 15th Street. I saw a man standing in the intersection and called for him to get out of the street. He said he didn't have to and took off running east on 15th Street.

I followed him in my police car until he cut through a yard and I started chasing him on foot. We went through several yards. After about two blocks I caught up to him, tackled him in an alley, and fell into a back yard off the alley. I got the cuffs on him and then stood him up. Looking around, I found I was in a back yard with about 20 guys having a beer and barbeque party. They were speaking Spanish and started to surround us.

Realizing I could be in big trouble, I called out, "Does anyone know this guy?" One person spoke up in English saying yes, they knew him. I yanked my cuffs off him and asked the fellow talking to me to please take care of him. As soon as I did that, I sensed a change in their attitudes. The guy I had talked with even tried to give me a beer. I thanked him but declined—all I could think about was getting the heck out of there, which I did.

That wasn't the last time I released a suspect. My attitude was that if making a misdemeanor arrest would create a larger problem, I'd let it go. There will always be another day. Looking back on it, I wondered why I even chased that guy. It isn't against the law to run and he wasn't a pedestrian in the roadway any longer. I think it's a basic reaction for a police officer that when someone runs, you assume they have done something wrong. It's the same way in vehicle pursuits. It is very difficult to not chase or pursue, but it's the right thing to do under certain circumstances.

An Ernie Hinkle Moment

Our name is one of the most important things we have. When we mispronounce someone's name, either accidentally or on purpose, it can cause a problem. The result is usually only confusion, but sometimes it is hurt feelings.

In supervising my troops, occasionally I pronounced a name wrong by accident and at other times, I did it on purpose to get someone's attention. "Toler" is not that common a surname which led to a great letter I got from Officer Fred "Dale" Toler on my birthday in 1982. Dale was a very dedicated officer and an asset to our platoon. On top of that, he could be pretty darn funny.

The letter, one of my most prized possessions, was inspired by what happened when I was talking to our platoon about radio procedures. Here's what Dale wrote:

Show-up in 1982 was both fun and stress-ful. As Patrol Officers, it was a time for either good-humored ribbing or a moment of supervi-sory encouragement (ass chewing). Being on the Spohnholtz/Hinkle (Charlie Patrol Shift) for al-most a year, I had not really experienced any-thing resembling the supervisory encouragement that other patrol shifts endured on a regular ba-sis. In looking back, it was not that the Charlie Patrol Shift was that good, but it had more to do with the competent leadership provided by both Capt. Spohnholtz and Lt. Hinkle.

Feeling like a veteran with almost one year on the streets, I walked into Show-up with al-most a John Wayne swagger and sat at my usual place on the back row near the door. The old Show-up Room was on the second floor of the Patrol Building with three-level, stadium-style seating looking down on a long table. Unknown to anyone on the shift, today was the day that all of the Spohnholtz/Hinkle (Charlie, Edward, and Baker Sectors) Patrol Shifts were to receive their supervisory encouragement. The topic of the encouragement is lost to time, but the mo-ment is burned into my memory as though it happened yesterday.

Sgt. Chuck Hickey read the announce-ments from the Show-up book with his usual monotone and lack of flair. I don't know why, but I do know that Police Sergeants are sup-posed to act almost robotic when making any Show-up announcements. Expressive emotions are strictly forbidden, lest the Sergeant appear weak and near the point of emotional break-down.

Upon completion of his highly informative announcements, Sgt. Hickey, in a very formal (first clue) manner asked (second clue) the other

Sergeants if they had anything to add. Sgt. Franks mumbled his affirmation and Sgt. Mathers nodded to the completion of Sgt. Hickey's reading. The floor now belonged to Lt. Hinkle. I believe Capt. Spohnholtz was present, but that's not relevant to the story.

Lt. Ernie Hinkle is a man who has, could and would chew out any Officer for a grievous mistake, but at the same time would treat the Officer as a human being. If you, as an Officer, really screwed up, at the end of his speech Lt. Hinkle would put his arm around you and hug (squeeze tightly), forcing most of the air out of your lungs. Then he would slap you on the back two or three times until all the (bad) air in your lungs had been expelled. As you struggled to regain your breath, Lt. Hinkle would smile and reaffirm his belief that you are a <u>good</u> Officer and that this mistake would never happen again. You know what? He was right 99% of the time!

I digress—now back to my most memorable Ernie Hinkle moment. Sitting in Show-up clueless to the upcoming supervisory encouragement we were about to receive, I sat there fat, dumb and happy thinking that I can't believe they pay me to drive fast and chase bad guys. So, I was wholly unprepared for Lt. Hinkle's next words:

"ALRIGHT... LISTEN UP... WHAT IS GOING ON HERE? ... ALL OF YOU KNOW BETTER THAN TO Blah... Blah... Blah... Blah... Blah..."

This went on for about five to ten minutes. As any of you who know Ernie Hinkle can attest, after a couple of minutes he began repeating himself or, I quit listening--that part is fuzzy. Hinkle had dressed down the entire three shifts, not speaking directly about any one person. But obviously, there was some important transgression that needed to be addressed immediately and severely. It's amazing how when you're a part of a large group being corrected, nothing hits you personally. So there I sat elevated by stadium seating high above Lt. Hinkle. At least that's what I thought.

Lt. Hinkle, no doubt feeling he was losing his captive audience's attention, must have started searching the group for the face of the oblivious. Like I said earlier, I had already quit listening. That's when he locked onto me or at least the space around me. Hinkle's wrath turned my direction and became very, very personal.

"TOLIVER, DO YOU THINK THIS IS FUNNY? ... No response ... WELL TOLIVER, I ASKED YOU, DO YOU THINK THIS IS FUNNY?"

Since Lt. Hinkle was obviously upset with someone around me, he had my full and undivided attention. Of course, since it was not me who was in trouble there probably was a smug grin planted on my face. While he waited for a response to his repeated questions, Lt. Hinkle's stare burned a hole through someone who was obviously standing too close to me. Again, Toliver gave no response. 'What the hell was this guy's problem?' I thought. Lt. Hinkle leaned as far forward as he could, cutting the distance in half.

"WELLLLLLL.............TOLIVER...?"

Now I'm thinking purely self-preservation at this time because whenever Toliver incinerates and turns to ash from Hinkle's stare, I don't even want a hint of a sunburn showing I was anywhere near the guy. Therefore, I look from side to side; nope, I know all of those guys. So, then I turn around to see if this lunatic Toliver is standing behind me. Much to my surprise there is no one behind me or even in the back of the room. Now you must understand that no one in the room has dared to move a muscle during this episode. While my head is turned away from Lt. Hinkle, I now belatedly realize Toliver is <u>ME</u>. If I could have gotten up and walked out of that room without facing Lt. Hinkle again, I certainly would have, but that's not reality.

I don't know why, but my smile grew in size enough that there was little that could disguise it. I slowly, and I mean ever so slowly, turned to face my Lieutenant for what surely would be the end of my life. When he looked at my face, no doubt the smile grabbed his attention. He levitated in his chair like an electric circuit was flowing through his body.

"WIPE THAT SMILE OFF OF YOUR FACE, TOLIVER!"

I wish it had been that easy, I could not for the life of me control the smile on my face. As a matter of fact, it grew larger and probably contorted my face. I was hoping Lt. Hinkle would think I was in pain and take pity on me.

"YOU KNOW WHO I'M TALKING TO. WIPE THAT SMILE OFF YOUR FACE…

TOLIVER!"

I'm not sure, but thinking about it now, I believe Lt. Hinkle realized his mispronunciation of my name. Because as quickly as this fixation had turned my direction, it ended, and the entire shift was thrown out of Show-up and ordered to hit the streets.

The Rest of the Story

The following day, before Show-up, Officer Wayne Simer had 30 stick-on nametags made, each with the name "Toliver." Everyone covered their real nametags with the stick-on. Capt. Spohnholtz, being a man to not let a good joke go to waste, lined up all three shifts for inspection. Lt. Hinkle, being an eagle-eyed Patrol Lieutenant of many years, passed only five Officers before he noticed the joke. To his credit, he laughed the loudest. This story has some hair on it; but, overall, the facts are correct. I will always look back on those years with fond memories.

Happy Birthday Lieutenant,
Fred (Dale) Toler

Description of a Police Officer

A reporter, Lindsey Lane, rode with our platoon on the night of Dec. 18, 1992 for a story she was working on about crime and how the police handled it. At the time, APD had been going through some turmoil. Several officers were in trouble because of their off-duty activities. Also, we were in the process of getting a new chief with Elizabeth Watson coming on board to replace Chief Jim Everett.

Ms. Lane interviewed several officers that night, including Doyne Bailey who offered a comment on what kind of officer I was -- a cross between Sheriff Andy Taylor on the Andy Griffin Show and John Wayne. Doyne really dropped it on me. I felt it was more like him describing himself.

Doyne later served as sheriff of Travis County for 12 years and then as director of the Governor's Office of Criminal

Justice for several years after that. He was very dedicated to the police profession and a role model for many officers.

Stopping a Jumper

In August 1982, the dispatcher broadcast a report of a man wearing a red shirt who had climbed over the guardrail at the 12th Street overpass above IH-35 and was about to jump. I was close to the location and the first officer to get there.

When I drove up, I saw a man with a red shirt in about the middle of the overpass on the north side. I parked on the frontage road and began to walk slowly toward him.

"Hey, partner," I called, "can I help you with anything?"

He denied anything was wrong. I saw a paper bag lying on the overpass near where he had climbed over. I looked in the bag and found he had left a one-page suicide note.

"Sir, you don't want to do this," I said. "Can I give you a ride anywhere?"

At that, he started crying and said, "I need some help." I assisted him back over the railing, put my arm around him, and walked him to my unit. I drove him to headquarters, got him some coffee, and arranged for him to talk to the police psychiatrist, Dr. Allen Deitz. Deitz was able to get him some help and, hopefully, things turned around for him.

Like the old saying goes, suicide is a long-term solution to a short-term problem.

Team Work Prevents Suicide

About 9 p.m. one evening in December 1992, officers responded to the 32nd Street overpass of IH-35 where a man was threatening to jump. Officers Joe Stanish and Don Doyle arrived and immediately took charge of the scene. They diverted traffic from the area and called for the lower-level traffic to be closed. They also began talking with the would-be jumper and kept him engaged while they tried to contact the department's crisis team.

I arrived at the scene, met with Sgt. Greg Lasley, and we had the man's father brought to the scene. But the despondent man said he didn't want to talk to his dad. Meanwhile, traffic was backing up for miles on IH-35 creating a dangerous situation.

Greg and I walked to where the other officers were talking with the subject and joined the conversation. After a while, we were able to gain his trust and slowly get nearer to him. I asked him not to hurt himself saying that we only wanted to help him. I also said that we were causing a dangerous traffic problem. By now we were pretty close to him and Lasley and I grabbed him and pulled him back over the railing.

As it turned out, the young man had quarreled with his girlfriend. His father, who had come to the scene, called the girlfriend and told her what was happening, but she refused to come to the scene. Not only that, she said she didn't care if he did jump. I suspect that relationship was over, but we had saved his life.

I was fortunate to have some success in preventing suicides, but saw too many cases with a far less favorable outcome which were all very sad. It got to the point where if I didn't need to make the scene of a suicide, I wouldn't go. I did come to realize that in most of the cases, the people had been calling out for help but didn't know how to get it.

One of the Bloodiest Knife Fights I Ever Saw

On March 16, 1991, I was patrolling in the 1400 block of West North Loop in front of the Fashion Aire Apartments when a young girl flagged me down. She was practically hysterical. I turned into the driveway and saw several people lying on the ground and others running in all directions. Blood was everywhere.

Someone had gone berserk with a butcher knife. By this time, Sgt. Greg Lasley with his wife, Cheryl (she was riding with him that shift), came to back me up. We followed the trail of blood to a second-story apartment. Inside, a man in his late 20s refused to open the door. We stood outside the door and talked to him and, after a little while, he surrendered. He had a large cut on his hand and we found a bloody knife in his apartment. He was taken to Brackenridge Hospital ER, got sewn up, and then went to jail.

Several of his victims went to the emergency room in serious condition. One man had cuts to his ear, jaw, neck, and shoulder. Another person had cuts to his left arm and lower back. Another guy, who obviously had been trying to run from the fight, ended up with a cut on both his left and right buttocks. A fourth person, who had no identification on him, had cuts all over his body. There were more people who got cut, but they refused treatment. I never found out what started the fight, but I have a suspicion it involved the young woman who had flagged me down.

Hostage by State Official

On the afternoon of Oct. 12, 1981, the sheriff's department notified APD that a deputy was working a hostage situation involving a taxi. The driver of Roy's Cab No. 180 had picked up a fare in the 2400 block of Ridge Circle in the Onion Creek Country Club area and the passenger was holding a gun on him.

I was driving north on IH-35 at Town Lake when the cab passed me. I turned on my vehicle's red lights and stopped the cab in the 700 block of East Frontage Road. As I approached the vehicle, I saw two people inside--the driver and another man in the back seat who had rolled a window down.

Since the call that went out said the passenger was armed, I grabbed him and pulled him out the window. He had been drinking and was pretty mouthy, so I handcuffed him. When I frisked him, I didn't find a weapon. The driver said he had picked the guy up at a private residence and told me he had never seen a gun.

All this happened fast; but, about this time, I realized the man was Bob Bullock, State Comptroller. I took the cuffs off him and told him that all I wanted to do was get to the bottom of this.

"Hell, yes," he said. "Let's get this over." He paid the cab driver and got in my unit. Bullock told me that he had taken a cab to his son's residence in Onion Creek. He had information that his son's roommate was using drugs and he didn't want his son to be around him. "I just wanted to run the son-of-a-bitch off," he told me. When I asked him if he had a gun in the cab, he looked at me and said, "Hinkle, just produce a gun." Then he asked if he was under arrest. I searched the cab for a gun but found nothing.

I checked with the deputy sheriff who had responded to the call and he said that he had not been able to find anyone in or around the house where the cab had picked up Bullock. I told the comptroller that he was not under arrest and that I was just following up on the initial report about a hostage in the cab.

Incidentally, when I took Bullock out of the cab, I accidentally tore his suit coat. I apologized for that and he said to forget it. By now, word was out that Bullock had been taken into custody, even though technically he had not been. When I got close to the police station, I saw several news vehicles parked outside, so I backed off and called Sgt. Jerry Staton to meet me.

Though Bullock had been drinking, he did not appear to be drunk and I had not found a gun on him or in the cab. In other words, I didn't have any reason to hold him. Saying he needed a drink, Bullock told me he wanted to go back to the Quorum Club in the 1200 block of Red River and I told the sergeant to take him there.

Later that night, I wrote a report describing what had happened.

The next day the American-Statesman ran a story on the incident. "I did no more than any father would have done," Bullock told a reporter. "I now consider the matter closed. I think all involved considers the matter closed. And, that is that."

He was right. That was that. I'm sure that Bullock had waved a pistol around that night, but he had managed to get rid of the weapon before I stopped that cab.

A few years later, about 11:30 p.m. one night, I stopped behind a vehicle for a red light at the intersection of Koenig Lane and North Lamar going westbound on Koenig Lane. The light changed to green but the car in front of me didn't move. It appeared to me the two occupants in the car were arguing and slapping at each other. The vehicle finally took off and I stopped it on the other side of the intersection. As I approached the driver's side of the car, I recognized Bullock.

"Hinkle, how in the hell are you," he said.

Surprised that he would remember my name, I asked him, "What is going on? Looks like you were fighting."

"Not a damn thing!" Bullock answered. "We are going home."

I could tell he was drinking so I asked him to get out of the car so I could conduct a sobriety test. He passed the test, but was very agitated at me. I sat him in my police car and talked to his wife. She said they had an argument but couldn't remember what it was over. She said they had just left a party and everything was okay now. She just wanted to go home.

I went back to my unit and talked to Bullock. I told him he shouldn't be drinking while driving and that one day it was going to slip up on him. I told him that he shouldn't put himself in that position. He then asked me if he was under arrest. I told him no and that he was free to go. He said, "It is about damn time," and he got out of the police unit slamming the car door behind him. He walked back to his car but then turned around, came back to my unit and said, "Thank you, Hinkle. I will think about your advice."

I told him, "Don't ever slam my car door again." He was pushing it.

Of course, Bullock later became Lieutenant Governor. He had treated me well but he had a well-deserved reputation for doing things his way. Despite that, Bob Bullock loved Texas. It showed in everything he did.

Ernie Hinkle

Who's Fastest?

I always tried to stay positive and do things that would make the troops laugh, like pulling pranks.

Rookies made easy targets. Whenever a newly commissioned officer got assigned to our platoon, I would meet with them to communicate what we expected out of them and listen to what they expected from us, trying always to put them at ease. Lastly, assuming we were getting more than one rookie, I would ask who the fastest runner in their group was. When they gave me a name, I would ask that person to meet me at a certain time on the back lot at the East Sub-Station on Springdale Road.

Thinking I was going to race them, they would be out there at the appointed time, but I would be nowhere around. After they had waited for a while, the sergeant on duty would arrive and tell them that I wasn't going to show up. He'd say that I just liked for the troops to know what great shape I was in. The next time I saw the rookie, I'd tell him he didn't have to prove anything to me, that if he said he was the fastest, I believed him.

Top Cop

My son, Ricky, earned a Top Cop fitness pin for being in the top 10 percent of physically fit APD officers. Since we had the same last name, his mailbox was just above mine. I saw the pin in his mailbox and decided to see how it looked on me. I borrowed it and wore it at all Show-ups, making sure that as many of the troops as possible saw it. Beyond that, I began shamelessly pointing out what great physical shape I was in and asking how many Top Cops we had on our platoon. It worked for a while until Ricky reported his pin missing and I got fieldstripped of my phony Top Cop status. Ricky finally got his pin back.

Precious Metal Dealer

I received a phone call from a man who said he was a professional in the precious metal business. He said police officers were harassing him and he wanted it stopped. When I asked him where his business was located, he told me it was in the area of East 7th Street and East Frontage Road.

Checking with officers working that area, I learned the caller was J. D., a local wino who often caused a traffic hazard by venturing out on the roadway to pick up aluminum cans he could sell to fund his supply of cheap wine.

I found J. D. a few days later and told him to keep his butt out of the streets. He was pushing a grocery basket about half full of cans. At least he was working. I saw him often and, for several years, he was always pushing that basket. He was quite a character and actually seemed to enjoy living on the streets. He had his monthly Social Security check mailed to the city jail as his permanent address.

Murder of a Prostitute

Over the years as a street lieutenant, I had to make the scene of way too many homicides. One thing I soon came to understand is that if an officer can't save someone's life, the best thing they can do for the victim is investigate the offense as thoroughly as possible.

Because of movies and TV, many citizens get the impression that plainclothes homicide detectives handle every aspect of a murder investigation, but that's not always the case. District uniform officers are usually the first on the scene of a murder. What they do when they get there is critical in finding the killer. Patrol officers protect the crime scene, identify witnesses if possible, take statements and photographs and prepare a detailed diagram showing the position of the body and what was around it. Homicide detectives also do these things, but they are not always on duty.

[213]

Around 3:30 a.m. on March 14, 1982, no homicide detectives were working when Officer Wayne Simer responded to an EMS call in the 1000 block of East 11th at Waller Street. On arrival, he found a man wearing women's clothing lying in a pool of blood along the south curb. The victim was pronounced dead at the scene ten minutes later.

I met Officer Simer at that location and made sure that the Medical Examiner's office and a police photographer had been called. Another officer on hand was Jerry Pierce who drew a diagram of the scene.

A hard-working cop and an excellent investigator, Simer had already located several witnesses. Sgt. Bill Alexander came by and took two of the witnesses to the police station to take statements from them. Through interviewing those witnesses and others, we learned that at least five shots had been fired at the victim by a short, thin man in his early 30s. After the shooting, the suspect ran down Waller Street, got in a white car, and sped off. Simer talked to someone who had seen the shooting. The witness didn't know the shooter by name, but thought he lived in the Hyde Park area.

Simer drove to a house in the 4500 block of Avenue A, but no one was there. From there, he took the witness to headquarters to take a statement from him.

Meanwhile, Officer Edward Robertson talked to a witness who identified the shooter as Olan Paz, a male with a goatee. At the police station, this witness identified Paz through a photo lineup conducted by Sgt. Alexander.

I took a statement at the scene from a woman who said the victim of the shooting was a friend of hers, a female impersonator whose street name was Marsha. They were prostitutes who had been standing on the corner of 11th and Waller when the suspect walked up to them and said, "Bitches, you took my money. I am going to kill you." Then he pulled a gun from his waistband. Seeing that, the witness started backing off. She'd walked about 15 feet when she heard a shot. Turning, she saw the man shoot her friend a second time. When he fell, the man went over and shot him another time.

After the shooting, the gunman took off running down Waller Street. The witness gave the same description we'd gotten from other witnesses, saying she had seen the shooter earlier in the night and could identify him if she saw him again.

Altogether, five officers, including me, had been at the scene or taking statements at headquarters. All our reports went to the homicide unit where the detectives took the case over the next morning.

Though it was not unusual to find men dressed like women (we called them "he-shes") working as prostitutes on East 11th and 12th Streets, it was hard to tell the difference until you got to know them.

As time would permit, I would patrol East 11th and 12th Streets east of IH-35 trying to cut down on prostitution and identify the he-shes. They were responsible for many assaults and were very good at picking pockets. I would pull up where they were standing and call them over to my unit. I'd get their name, ask where they worked when they weren't on the streets, and ask also about their families. I found out they usually worked in pairs—one he-she and a female. I never fully trusted them but, from time to time, I did get some good information about who was doing what on the streets.

My wife's father, Arthur Bailey, occasionally rode with me on the night shift when he came to visit us. He was in his 70s, a fine man, and I enjoyed having him with me. As time permitted, I would drive him down 11th Street so he could see the prostitutes standing around. I'd suggest that he look close to see if he could tell a he-she from a female. Arthur said they all looked like women to him.

One time I stopped at 11th and Curve Streets to talk to two prostitutes. As I stopped, Arthur asked, "How are you boys doing tonight?" They tried to convince Arthur they were women, but Arthur had them correctly pegged as guys in drag.

An Amazing Honor and a Humbling Experience

I was working the 3 p.m. to 1 a.m. shift on January 7, 1994 when I got a call from Capt. Rick Coy, then supervisor of the Police Academy and Training Facility. The captain asked if I could meet him at about 6:30 p.m. at the Lyndon Baines Johnson Library auditorium. He said the 83rd Cadet Class was graduating at 7 p.m. and that Chief Elizabeth Watson wanted a street officer to welcome the new cadets to the department.

Rick and I had worked on the same platoon together for more than two years and were good friends. Because of that, I wasn't shy about asking if he couldn't send another officer. But he made it plain that even though he had asked me, it was an order. I "cowboyed up" and told him I would be there.

When I arrived at the auditorium, the captain met me and took me down to the front row to sit with the academy instructors. I noticed Lt. Ceil Hart sitting with Chief Watson and the other dignitaries on the stage. Seeing the lieutenant, I felt a little relief. Maybe Rick, who would be the emcee during the ceremony, had changed his mind and had asked Lt. Hart to welcome the new officers.

I counted 38 cadets waiting to receive their commissions in the packed auditorium. After Mayor Bruce Todd and cadet class President Michael Jacques made their talks and before Chief Watson gave the oath of office, Capt. Coy said, "Our department had several role models and one officer here tonight fits that description." After reading information from the Police Awards Committee, he called me to the podium and announced that from then on one member of each graduating cadet class—chosen by their classmates—would be given the Ernie Hinkle Humanitarian Award.

The captain said the first award would go to Cadet Daniel Armstrong. He then called Armstrong to the podium and I had the honor of presenting him with the plaque.

All this caught me totally off guard. When I saw my wife and our entire family (including grandkids) along with some special family friends sitting on the opposite side of the auditorium, I knew it was a setup with me having been the only guy not clued in. I somewhat broke down—the tears were flowing. My son, Ricky, was on the department at that time and had sure kept this quiet and Capt. Coy had pulled it off without a hitch. I am very blessed and humbled by the honor of having this award named after me.

Sometime later, I asked the captain just how the Humanitarian Award came about. He said Chief Watson and her staff wanted to recognize an officer who had a history of helping others and who had brought credit to the department and the City of Austin. The Awards Committee, staff, and a civilian, Floyd McDowell, had reviewed all officers' 201 Files (personnel files) and interviewed a number of individuals. He said that my name kept coming up and that my 201 File was packed with complimentary memos and thank you letters.

McDowell later told me he had seen numerous complimentary letters in my file from people I had ticketed who still appreciated the way I had treated them. I told him those letters were the exception and not the rule. I was more likely to get my butt chewed out by indignant motorists than an attaboy letter.

Looking over my 201 File, which the department gave me after I retired, the majority of the letters in it had to do with me just doing my job, the same as any officer would have done. Remembering the smile on a little boy's face when I found his stolen bicycle, how people looked when I bought gas for someone who had run out of gas and didn't have any money, or providing dinner for someone down on his luck, meant more to me than pieces of paper, though I certainly appreciated the "thank you" letters. More than once, I spent my lunch money to help someone out, so thank goodness for Dunkin' Donuts and other businesses that sold donuts or food at half-price to police officers. At times, I took advantage of it. And sometimes, people actually paid me back by sending money to me through the police department. Here are a few examples of letters and memos from my file:

Ernie Hinkle

1-19-89

Ernie Hinkle—

We are returning the money you so generously gave when we needed gas. Thanks for helping us out Tuesday night (1-17-89). You really saved us from a long walk. Once again Thank you very, very much.

Your Friends

Dear officer Hinkle,

Sorry it took me so long to return this to you. I really appreciate your help getting my car unlocked. You made a bad situation good. I hope you have a great holiday.

Thanks very much

Brenda Frank

Got slim jim stuck in her car door and couldn't get it out in aug. 90 Like returned it for Christmas 12-25-90 Ernie Hinkle

---

City of Austin
TELEPHONE MESSAGE

To: Lt. ERNIE HINKLE
1/27/89
date   am · pm

DIANE KLEIN

Of
Phone Number

Phoned		Please call	
Came to see you		Will call again	
Outside to see you		Returned your call	

Message THANK YOU VERY MUCH FOR YOUR HELP THURSDAY NIGHT. I GREATLY APPRECIATED IT. THANK YOU AGAIN. $5.00

DIANE

(Person receiving call)

GSD 4008 (6/80)
CSN 753-14-52-048   Over

[218]

Since APD first established the Ernie Hinkle Humanitarian Award in 1994, the department has subsequently graduated 44 cadet classes. The 127th Cadet Class graduated May 30, 2014. Chief Art Acevedo and his staff have been very faithful in inviting me to present the award when other obligations don't keep me from doing so. At the last graduation I attended, Commander Phillip Crochet introduced me:

"It is an honor and a delight to introduce to you Retired APD Lieutenant Ernie Hinkle who

will present the Humanitarian Award. Lt. Hinkle was the Class President of the 23rd Cadet Class, commissioned on September 30, 1960. He spent his entire career as a street officer. Lt. Hinkle promoted to Line Lieutenant in 1973, where he remained for 22 years because he so enjoyed people and did not want to leave Patrol.

At one time, Lt. Hinkle was the most decorated police officer in the City of Austin. Among his many merits and over 200 awards and commendations, in 1993 he was one of 18 law enforcement officers in the State of Texas to be selected by the Commission on Law Enforcement to receive a Law Enforcement Achievement Award for Professional Achievement.

Retiring on November 25, 1995, Lt. Hinkle devoted more than 35 years of his life to the Austin Police Department, giving unselfishly of himself to others each and every day of his career.

Now retired, he remains in our hearts and minds as the symbol of what a great officer should be –

Ernie Hinkle

Courageous, but kind;
Honorable, but humble;
Principled, but with a deep understanding
of the frailty of the human condition.

Ladies and gentlemen, Lieutenant Ernie Hinkle."

Ernie Hinkle (left) presenting Gonzalo Vivas the 'Ernie Hinkle Humanitarian Award' May 17, 2013.

Proud Moments

There were some very proud and special moments for me after my retirement. On January 23, 1996, my son, Ricky, asked me to pin his badge on when he was promoted to lieutenant. He retired in 2009 as a commander. Rick had the respect of all who knew him.

I was also asked to pin on the badge of my son-in-law, Todd Smith, when he was promoted to sergeant. He is now a lieutenant doing a great job.

I was again honored to make a presentation to the 115th Cadet Class graduating on January 2, 2009, when my grandson-in-law, John Majefski, graduated from the academy. He is doing a great job and is well liked by everyone.

We are definitely a law enforcement family. But whenever we can all get together, we just enjoy being together as a family, having fun, and sharing our love for each other. Would you believe we hardly ever, if ever, talk about police work when we are together?

Influences on Rank and File

If a bricklayer tells another bricklayer he is doing a good job, that compliment is very rewarding because they are in the same profession. I was greatly influenced by many of the officers I worked with learning much more from them than they ever did from me.

Looking back on my career, I had many role models. Some were officers who just wanted to stay on the streets and not promote. What a delight it was for me to see other role models move up in the ranks and promote to commanders and assistant chiefs, then retire and become chiefs of police at other departments. Some examples (to just name a few):

- James Fealy - Chief of Police, High Point, North Carolina.
- Robert Dahlstrom - Chief of Police, University of Texas in Austin
- Duane McNeill - Chief of Police, Canon City, Colorado
- John Neff - Chief Deputy Sheriff, Llano County, Texas
- Harold Piatt - Chief of Police, Cottonwood, Texas
- Gary Olfers - Constable, Precinct 1, Horseshoe Bay, Texas
- Howard Williams – Chief of Police, San Marcos, Texas

There are so many more I have lost contact with over the years.

Retirement

In early 1995 at almost 63 years of age, I began to think about retiring. I was still working the streets and my health was good, but I knew I could no longer keep up with the younger officers. Also, they installed a computer in my car, Unit 202. I was having trouble reading the computer, listening to my radio, being on the cell phone, and driving the car, all at the same time. I believe the term is "multi-tasking."

The fact is, I was "old school," and modern technology was taking over. With the new equipment, I could stop a vehicle, run the plates to see if it had been reported as stolen, and have the information back before the vehicle pulled off. Those are great tools for law enforcement, but it took some time for me to get efficient with it.

I also thought about my dad still working in his 80s. On the other hand, I still enjoyed going to work and retiring was still just something I figured I would do someday.

In 1993, we had bought a house on the water at Horseshoe Bay near Marble Falls in Llano County. My friend, Capt. Spohnholtz, had retired and lived at Sunrise Beach just across the lake from our house. The captain and I were the best of friends after working together for two decades. We fished together a lot, and were always there for each other. During 1995, I spent a lot of time at the lake working on the house and fishing with Gerald.

Realizing that we would be moving to Horseshoe Bay after I retired made the difference in deciding if I would retire. In early November 1995, I turned in my paperwork to retire effective November 25th. But, when I took off my uniform and changed into regular attire, I realized that not going to work was going to be a challenge for me. I quickly missed the streets, but not as much as I missed my fellow officers.

In February 1996, my wife and family pulled off a surprise retirement party for me. Turns out that my wife had talked to former Austin Mayor Roy Butler who graciously insisted on hosting the event at his beer distributorship's hospitality room at no cost to the family. He was always a strong supporter of the department and, when he was mayor, I had a lot of contact with him. He was a good friend.

To get me to the party without my knowing it was for me, my wife asked my daughter to tell me she was getting an award at work and it was important to her that I be there for her. On the evening of the party, my wife drove us to the Capitol Beverage Company. Discovering a large crowd gathered in my honor was a huge surprise, especially to an old cop who prided himself in always knowing what was going on, especially within my own family. Most of my old shift and many friends and family members were there. It was a roast, and I ended up "well done."

"Honor, courtesy, and at all times fair dealings in the matter of the Austin Police Department." These words are posted on the walls at the Police Academy and I tried to live by them during my 35 years on the job. I am indebted to my fellow officers, civilian personnel and the other law enforcement agencies I had the privilege of working with. They all contributed greatly to my career and I am honored to have had the opportunity to work with them. My thanks to the City of Austin and the State of Texas for the faith allotted me to serve them.

Ernie Hinkle

It has been a beautiful life. Beth and I enjoy living on Lake LBJ and enjoy being with our wonderful family and friends. And, fishing is not too bad either.

I enjoyed my career as a police officer and was fortunate in so many ways. God was with me and I am so very thankful for that and so proud to be an American.

Once a person puts the badge on, it never seems to come off. There will always be a fellowship in law enforcement that goes on in one's life after retirement. Even after being retired for almost 19 years, there is a longing for the old days, the adrenaline that flowed, and for the camaraderie with people I worked with and respected. I will always be a cop at heart.

PICTURES, LETTERS
AND AWARDS

Officer Ernie Hinkle directing traffic
on 6th Street and Congress 1962

*Lt. Ernie Hinkle and Lt. Roosevelt Sampson manning the
City of Austin Booth at the Motorola Orientation at Palmer
Auditorium in 1974.*

CITY OF BOSTON  MASSACHUSETTS

KEVIN H. WHITE
MAYOR

February 7, 1974

Dear Ernie:

Your performance was among the finest and
most gracious I have ever seen and I can't thank
you enough for your hospitality, warmth, and
friendliness. You helped to make my visit to
Austin a pleasant memory.

I know that letters like this sound routine
and I know an offer to drop by is often an expected reciprocation for courtesies extended;
but I sincerely want you to know that I would
be offended if you don't make it a point to
visit me in Boston.

Sincerely,

Kevin H. White
Mayor

Lieutenant Ernie Hinkel
Police Department
City Hall
Austin, Texas

City of Austin

Founded by Congress, Republic of Texas, 1839
Police Department, 715 East 8th Street, Austin, Texas 78701-3397 Telephone 512/480-5005

October 15, 1984

Mrs. George W. Cowden
Chairman
Board of Trustees

Dear Mrs. Cowden:

When I received the nomination form from Captain Louie White of
our Community Services Division, it brought to mind one of our
most outstanding officers. He is Lieutenant Ernie Hinkle of the
Patrol Bureau with the Austin Police Department.

Lt. Hinkle works each and every day attempting to better the
lives of individuals in need. Since starting with our Department
in January of 1961, he has performed in such an outstanding
manner that I doubt that the combined careers of any other three
(3) officers would equal his efforts. He has received recognition
for life saving on three (3) different occasion, six (6) Police
Commendation Bars, four (4) Certificates of Merit and three (3)
Meritorious Conduct Bars.

This individual cousels and assists individuals under the most
trying circumstances when a traumatic experience has just
occurred. He has talked people out of committing suicide and
criminals into surrendering--thus saving their lives.

There are several memos and other information for your
consideration. Please feel free to call me should you desire any
further data. Thank you for the opportunity to submit the name
of a really worthy individual.

Sincerely,

George Phifer
Assistant Chief of Police

GP/cm

ADMIN7

The Counseling and Pastoral Care Center of Austin cele-brating its Ten Outstanding Persons of 1986: (In alphabet-ical order) Billye Brown, Malcom L. Cooper, Wilhelmina Ruth Fitzgerald Delco, Reverend A. D. Eberhart, Gustavo L. Garcia, Lieutenant Ernie Hinkle, Ronya Kozmetsky, Janet Ray Poage, Bert Kruger Smith, and Ann White.

1991 APD Supervisor of the Year Award presented to Lt. Ernie Hinkle by Chief George Phifer.

1992 - Lt. Hinkle with Elizabeth Hinkle receiving the Austin City Council Award.

123 N. Ingleside Drive
Fayetteville, NC 28303
July 18, 1993

Dear Lt. Hinkle,

I want to thank you for your part in my summer internship with APD. Out of all the things we did I enjoyed riding with the officers on your shift more than anything. You and your shift made us feel very welcome and actually let us get involved. The officers that I specifically rode with were all very accommodating. Officer Sam Ramirez introduced me to all the transients downtown and also the neighborhood 7-11 where I learned about the free drinks that would be a Godsend during the shifts I rode. And Jesse Severson showed me how to run a warrant and how to make breakfast tacos all in one day! Officer David New showed me how fast-paced Charlie sector could be but he never found any crack for me to see unfortunately. And finally Officer Tim Ritzenthaler who drove me all over David sector looking for something but even the calls we got were over before we got there. But nevertheless I enjoyed every minute of every day I rode with these officers. Working with APD has been a very rewarding experience for me. I thoroughly enjoyed meeting and working with you, Lt. Hinkle. I can see exactly why everyone told me that you were the best of the best. Thank you once again.

With warmest regards,
Michele Sada
UNC - Chapel Hill

My thanks to you all
for representing us so
well!
Ray Sanders 8-12-93

1993 State of Texas Law Enforcement
Law Enforcement
Professional Achievement Award

IN GRATEFUL APPRECIATION OF HIS CONTRIBUTIONS TO

THE CITIZENS OF THE STATE OF TEXAS

IN THE FIELD OF LAW ENFORCEMENT

LIEUTENANT ERNIE W. HINKLE, JR.

IS AWARDED

THE PROFESSIONAL ACHIEVEMENT AWARD

BY THE STATE OF TEXAS

ON THIS THE 13TH DAY OF MAY, IN THE YEAR OF OUR LORD, 1993

John Hannah Jr
JOHN HANNAH, JR.
SECRETARY OF STATE

Retirement November 25, 1995 -
Elizabeth and Ernie Hinkle with Mike Lummas

KVET-KASE BROADCASTING COMPANY, INC.

THE KVET-KASE BUILDING
POST OFFICE BOX 380
AUSTIN, TEXAS 78767

512-495-1300

December 14, 1995

Lt. Ernie Hinkle
Austin Police Department
715 East 8th Street
Austin, Texas 78701

Dear Ernie:

I am told you are retiring this week-end from a long and distinguished career in the Austin Police Department.

As a former Mayor, and as a citizen of Austin, I want to both thank you and congratulate you for the dedicated service you have rendered to the citizens of Austin for all these years.

You are a role model for all officers to come.

Respectfully,

Roy Butler
Chairman of the Board

cc: Chief Elizabeth Watson

THREE OF THE MOST POWERFUL VOICES IN TEXAS

**OFFICE OF THE
DISTRICT ATTORNEY**

P.O. Box 1748 · Austin 78767
Telephone 512/473-9400
Telefax 512/473-9695

RONALD EARLE
DISTRICT ATTORNEY

STEPHEN McCLEERY
FIRST ASSISTANT

December 15, 1995

Lieutenant Ernie W. Hinkle, Jr.
Austin Police Department
Austin, Texas 78701

Dear Ernie:

I had looked forward to being with you today, but unless this virus
that I have gets better, I will probably not be able to be there.
I can't talk, and being a public official without a voice is like
being in a gunfight without a gun.

It has been almost 26 years since I first met many of you, and we
looked a little different then. That was a formative period for
me, as it no doubt was for you; the experiences that young people
have often mark the course of much of their later lives.

That has certainly been true for me. Knowing and working with
officers of the Austin Police Department as a municipal judge
shaped the course of my life. The lessons I learned with you and
from you influence decisions that I make everyday. I want to thank
you for that. It was the finest education available anywhere.

I also want to thank you on behalf of the community for which we
both work for your service to all of us.

Over the years law enforcement has been called on to perform more
and more of the functions that the family and the neighborhood
performed 25 years ago. I have seen the toll it has taken on you
to be the glue that holds it all together.

In return, you hold a special place in the hearts of the people of
this beloved community. You carry with you the gratitude and
respect of many, many people.

It has been a pleasure working with you. I look forward to future
visits.

Sincerely,

Ronald Earle

*I sure do,
miss you!*

Made in the USA
Lexington, KY
22 March 2015